GETTING IT RIGHT
RIGHT
This
Time

How to Create
a Loving
and
Lasting
Marriage

Barry and

D1057342

Routledge
Taylor & Francis Group
New York   London

Published in 2006 by
Routledge
Taylor & Francis Group
270 Madison Avenue
New York, NY 10016

Published in Great Britain by
Routledge
Taylor & Francis Group
2 Park Square
Milton Park, Abingdon
Oxon OX14 4RN

Printed in the United States of America on acid-free paper
10 9 8 7 6 5 4 3 2 1

International Standard Book Number-10: 0-415-95169-0 (Softcover)
International Standard Book Number-13: 978-0-415-95169-2 (Softcover)
Library of Congress Card Number 2005014280

Library of Congress Cataloging-in-Publication Data

McCarthy, Barry W., 1943-
    Getting it right this time : how to create a loving and lasting marriage / by Barry McCarthy, Emily J. McCarthy.
        p. cm.
    ISBN 0-415-95169-0 (pbk.)
    1. Remarriage. 2. Stepfamilies. 3. Remarried people--Family relationships. 4. Divorced people--Family relationships. I. McCarthy, Emily J. II. Title.

HQ1018.M33 2005
306.84--dc22   2005014280

Taylor & Francis Group
is the Academic Division of Informa plc.

Visit the Taylor & Francis Web site at
http://www.taylorandfrancis.com

and the Routledge Web site at
http://www.routledge-ny.com

GETTING IT
RIGHT
This
Time

CONTENTS

CHAPTER 1   What Happened to "Happy Ever After"?   1

CHAPTER 2   The Courage to Divorce   17

CHAPTER 3   Learning From the Past   33

CHAPTER 4   Choosing Well   45

CHAPTER 5   Money and Second Marriage   61

CHAPTER 6   Intimacy and Sexuality   75

CHAPTER 7   Stepfamilies and Stepparenting—
Yours, Mine, and Ours   89

CHAPTER 8   Should We Have a Child?   103

CHAPTER 9   Traps and Vulnerabilities   115

CHAPTER 10   Understandings and Agreements   129

CHAPTER 11   Dealing With the Ex-Spouse   143

CHAPTER 12   The Imperfect Marriage—
              Surviving Hard Times   155

CHAPTER 13   Marriage After 50   169

CHAPTER 14   Cost-Benefit Assessment of Difficult
              Marriages   183

CHAPTER 15   Pride and Acceptance   197

APPENDIX A   Choosing an Individual, Couple, or Family
              Therapist   203

APPENDIX B   Marriage and Stepfamily Support Groups
              and Enhancement Programs   205

APPENDIX C   Recommended Books   207

CHAPTER 1

What Happened to "Happy Ever After"?

When you grew up, what was considered the most important choice in life (especially for women)? Whom you married. It was love at first sight and happy ever after. A generation ago the average age at which couples married was 23 for males and 21 for females, although many married right after high school (especially when the woman was pregnant). Marriage was the secure foundation, and life revolved around it.

What happened to the myth of "happy ever after"? It never matched reality. People have divorced throughout history. The United States has one of the highest divorce rates in the world. Everyone knows someone (family, friend, coworker, neighbor) who has been divorced. Approximately 40 percent of first marriages end in divorce. The divorce rate is even higher for second marriages, more than 60 percent, and it is higher still for subsequent marriages (especially after the fourth). Should we give up on marriage?

When marriage works well it meets the needs for intimacy and stability better than any other relationship. However, the loneliest, most depressed people are not single or divorced people but those trapped in fatally flawed or abusive marriages. Marriage can enhance your psychological well-being or subvert it. Marriage is not healthy if it is just a symbol without real substance. The crucial factor is maintaining a satisfying relationship and commitment to a stable marriage.

Clinicians' offices are full of married people who say their problem is a dysfunctional marriage; if only they were not married to this person life would be fine. Single people tell the clinician that all their problems would be solved by marriage. However, it is not marriage per se that enhances well-being, but whether marriage is healthy, satisfying, and stable. With a marital bond based on respect, trust, and intimacy, marriage enhances self-esteem and promotes life satisfaction. You are better single or divorced than in an abusive, disrespectful, non-trusting, or non-intimate marriage.

People's lives and relationships are more complex and multidimensional than the "yes–no" measure of whether a marriage endures or ends in divorce. Marriage therapy does not guarantee the outcome; rather, it facilitates the process by which a couple examines and attempts to change its relationship. This process involves communication, power, roles, attraction, parenting, sexuality, problem-solving, and conflict management. The hope is that the persons involved can resolve problems and revitalize their marital bond. However, in a significant number of cases there is a basic incompatibility that results in a fatally flawed marriage. Other couples find that the bond has been irreparably broken. No degree of therapeutic intervention, wishful thinking, prayer, or family pressure can restore it. For some couples there is "too much water over the dam"—financial stress, bitterness about an affair, resentment over abusive incidents, distrust over broken promises, anger over a move—respect and trust have been destroyed. All couples experience stressful periods in which their relationships are strained and frayed. As long as you think of yourselves as "we" the marriage can be revitalized. However, when the bond is broken, it is difficult, if not impossible, to resurrect the marriage.

The Courage to Leave

Studies of divorce demonstrate that it is a most stressful life event. This stress does not ebb over a matter of days or weeks. The divorce process evolves over one to three years. It takes courage to confront the sad reality that the marriage is not viable and act to end this chapter in your life. Most relationships require a crisis to impel the move to divorce—discovery of an affair, a humiliating incident, an out-of-control fight, a child acting out. Choosing to divorce is painful. It is hard to sit across the kitchen table from a person whom you promised two or twenty-two years ago to love and care for through good times and bad and admit the marriage has failed. It takes courage to face the harsh reality that you are not a respectful, trusting, intimate couple. Breaking apart in angry, hurtful ways over a specific crisis or transgression makes this easier.

An adage in marital therapy is that one person cannot save a marriage. Marriage is a joint effort. An adage in divorce therapy is that divorce is seldom a mutual decision. It is easier to be the person who leaves than the person who is left, at least initially.

The United States is a culture in which women leave marriages more than men. More than 75 percent of divorce decisions are initiated by women. The most common reason is that the woman no longer respects or trusts her mate. Traditionally it was the woman's role to hold together the marriage and family, whatever the cost. Divorce requires an inner strength and ability to tolerate family, religious, and community disapproval. The stigma of divorce has decreased over the past generation, which is a healthy development. However, the stigma still exists, especially for the woman. Her standard of living will probably decline, partly because many men do not maintain child support commitments or involvement with parenting. Being a single mother is not easy, but women have learned to care enough about their emotional well-being and that of their children to leave a destructive or abusive marriage.

The most common reason for males leaving a marriage is for another woman. The emotional and sexual bond is dead, and an affair is used as a transition to separation. The high risk of an affair becoming a second marriage is discussed elsewhere, but the affair serves as an impetus to confront the state of the current marriage. Although couples can and do recover from affairs, the affair (whether engaged in by the wife or husband) can be a statement that this is a non-viable marriage. Sexuality is a prime means of energizing the marital bond. A dysfunctional, unsatisfying, or non-existent sexual relationship is a severe drain on a marriage. The three major issues causing divorce are difficulties around money, sex, and children. The person seeking the divorce has the courage to confront the lack of emotional and sexual intimacy and chooses to terminate the relationship rather than settle for a loveless, sex-less marriage.

There are no perfect people and no perfect marriages. All marriages have weaknesses and vulnerabilities. There is a vast difference in accepting a spouse with his or her strengths and weaknesses, and settling for a marriage that is depressed, chaotic, abusive, or empty because it is the "right" or "socially desirable" thing to do.

Who We Are and the Plan of This Book

Emily and Barry McCarthy have spent 5 years researching and writing this book, the ninth book they have coauthored. Barry is a practicing Ph.D. clinical psychologist, a professor of psychology, and a certified marital and sex therapist. Emily has a degree in speech communication. A previous book, *Getting It Right the First Time*, focused on the rewards and challenges of a first marriage.

Ours is a first marriage, a bond that has endured for 38 years. Why should a couple in a first marriage be writing a book about second or subsequent marriages? A theme of our books, whether the topic is marriage or sex, is taking responsibility and making decisions that enhance your well-being and the lives of those you care about. Accepting the reality of divorce and affirming it as a positive choice rather than a personal failure is central to this theme. Positive motivation promotes wise decision-making in the present and future. Low self-esteem, guilt, or shame about the past subverts life and relationships.

In Barry's clinical practice, as well as in conducting workshops on marriage, marital therapy, and sex therapy, and in review-ing empirical and clinical research, the core importance of self-esteem and healthy relationships is clear. Barry cautions divorced people against engaging in "what-if" thinking or "beating up" on themselves about the divorce. Accept the sad reality of the divorce, learn from it, and focus on the present and future.

There are two crucial challenges that emanate from a divorce. The first is to identify vulnerabilities and traps so they do not control your life and the potential of a subsequent marriage. The second is the commitment to create a second marriage and family that are satisfying and stable. These will be the major themes of this book.

Awareness is necessary but not sufficient. Good intentions are not enough. You need a specific plan to monitor traps and ensure that positive learning is implemented. You need the active involvement and support of your current spouse. The "common sense" advice to keep potential problems to yourself so they do not interfere with this marriage is not only wrong but can be destructive. Marriage is based on a respectful, trusting relationship. You share weaknesses and seek support from your spouse. In our marriage, we shared personal vulnerabilities from our families of origin (neither parental model was a positive one) and from problems and disappointments earlier in our marriage. Our bond of respect, trust, and intimacy has grown stronger. In this book we will guide you in applying these ideas in your own life.

The audience for this book are people who are divorced, contemplating a second marriage, or in a second or subsequent marriage. This material is relevant in relationships involving one person's first marriage and the other's second. We present information, guidelines, case studies, and exercises. This is not a do-it-yourself therapy book; nor does it pretend to offer perfect advice that will work for everyone. Human behavior has many dimensions. Barry's clinical work has taught him to respect individual, couple, cultural, and value differences. Each person and couple assumes responsibility for their lives and marriage. Knowledge is power. The greater your awareness and commitment to utilize positive resources, the better able you are to make decisions that promote happiness and a satisfying, stable second marriage.

This book is not meant to be read like a novel. Rather, each chapter is self-contained and stands alone. Read chapters that are relevant to your situation. Most chapters include a case study. These are composite cases of clients Barry has seen in his practice, with names and details altered to protect confidentiality. Case studies demonstrate that "normal couples" have problems that can be resolved. They illustrate the variety of psychological, relational, and situational causes of problems. People change and relationships improve. The problems and solutions sound easy in a three-page summary, but, in fact, changes take time and commitment. There is seldom a smooth, miraculous cure.

Most chapters contain an exercise. The exercise provides a format to apply concepts in a concrete, personal way. Do not view exercises as required homework or something you are forced to do by this book or your partner. Do an exercise only if you think it could be helpful to you. Use the exercise structure to promote awareness and change. In discussing concepts and exercises, we suggest the following feedback guidelines.

1. Be constructive and caring; use at least three positive reinforcers for each negative comment.
2. Give positive feedback before a negative comment.
3. Be specific.
4. Request the change you want and avoid making negative comments about the spouse's personality, background, or family.
5. Support the spouse in making the changes you request.

Confronting Stigma

Divorce is now more frequent, but not more popular. Divorce is not a good thing; people do not get married with the intention of getting divorced. It still is not socially acceptable, although its stigma has lessened. Pejorative phrases like "broken families," "failed marriages," "the shame of divorce," "what will people think about dating a divorcee," have dramatically decreased. The not-so-funny joke is that second divorces now have the stigma first divorces had a generation ago.

Divorce is a healthy alternative to a fundamentally flawed, abusive, or destructive marriage. Divorced people cannot allow themselves to feel mired in stigma; it is unfair and untrue. It took wisdom to recognize that the marriage was not viable and courage to act on that reality. You need not be ashamed, guilty, or apologetic about having divorced. Sadness and regret are more reasonable and healthy reactions.

Although people talk about the epidemic of divorce as if it were a new phenomenon, the truth is that the divorce rate in the United States began rising in the early 1900s. Divorce peaked right after World War II, decreased in the 1950s, rose to new levels in the 1970s, and has remained high, although it is no longer growing. Approximately 40 percent of first marriages end in divorce. Is this a sign of "moral decay," as fundamentalist ministers charge? Or is it a complex multidimensional phenomenon, as the social and behavioral scientists maintain? Not surprisingly, we support the latter view.

In traditional cultures, the institution of marriage is rigidly supported by law, religion, community, and extended family. In some countries divorce is illegal or extremely difficult to obtain. Traditionally, marriage was based on the male-dominant model that assigned rigid, separate roles to the man and woman. The male worked and was in control of discipline, while the woman was responsible for the children, house, and taking care of the man. This model promoted stable marriages, but at a terrible cost. It did not provide for healthy or satisfying marriages. Rather, it subverted the happiness of family members, especially women. Few mental health professionals support the traditional, rigid model of marriage.

In understanding the high U.S. divorce rate, five factors come into play:

1. Greater economic freedom, especially for women.
2. Laws making divorce easier and less punitive.
3. Reduced religious, community, and family stigma.
4. Changing roles of men and women.
5. Promotion of psychological well-being and satisfying marriages, with less tolerance for abusive, dysfunctional, or marginal marriages.

These are healthy trends, not bad ones. Traditionally, poor or marginal marriages were tolerated and bolstered by the stigma of divorce and religious, community, and extended family pressure. Marriages that could not stand on their own endured, often at great cost to both the adults and children. Inherently unsound marriages were acceptable because the woman was supposed to "do the right thing" and avoid the stigma of a "broken family." Divorce was viewed as "selfish."

We must avoid going back to the rigid model of marital stability at any cost. Marriages can be both satisfying and stable. We are very pro-marriage. We believe in marriages that are respectful, trusting, intimate, and committed. Marriage promotes the life fulfillment of adults and children. The most important relationship in a family is the husband–wife bond. Functional, satisfying marriages promote functional, satisfying families. The well-being of children is promoted by healthy marriages. Whether the couple stays together or divorces is less important than whether the family provides a healthy environment for children to grow up. "Staying together for the sake of the children" has not been supported by empirical studies, especially in families where there is a high level of conflict or violence. Children are not helped by seeing parents fight, abuse one another, or be hateful. Children do prefer to grow up in an intact family, but not in a high-conflict, chaotic family.

The Value of a Second Marriage

The majority of people who divorce will remarry—approximately 85 percent of men and 65 percent of women. For people who divorce before age 40, those percentages are higher. People give up on the failed marriage but not on the hope for an intimate, stable marriage. The decision to divorce is a commitment to a healthier life, both for yourself and your children. The failed marriage made you deeply unhappy, and you deserve better, including the hope for a happy, secure second marriage and stepfamily.

People enter a first marriage with the naive belief that "love is enough" and that nothing will interfere with "happy ever after." Unfortunately, first marriage often involves marrying the wrong person for the wrong reasons. You idealize the spouse and view the relationship as perfect. Wrong reasons to marry include an unplanned pregnancy, rescue from loneliness, fear you will never find someone to marry if you say no to this opportunity, desire to get away from home or a bad living situation, the need to prove something to yourself or someone else, because friends are getting married, pressure from family, or because you do not know what else to do. Naïve motivation is less likely in a second marriage. However, be aware of negative motivations, especially proving to someone else (often the ex-spouse) that you can find someone to remarry.

Positive motivations promote positive outcomes. Remarry only if you believe this marriage will meet needs for intimacy and security. If it meets important needs—a mother for your children, financial security, a nicer house, a new start, a supportive extended family, child care, a companion to go places with, opportunity for travel—that is great, but these should not be substitutes for respect, trust, and intimacy. A woman who married for wealth said ruefully, "I earned every penny—living in a wealthy, abusive house is no better than living in a financially strapped, non-communicative marriage." All the practical, socially acceptable reasons to remarry will not compensate for a second marriage that is fundamentally troubled.

Can second marriages be successful? Empirically, the majority of people in a stable second marriage are happier than in the first marriage. Age and experience facilitate self-awareness and better decision-making. Learning from the first marriage and making a commitment to devote time and energy to ensure a successful second marriage is vital. Partner choice in a second marriage is better; there is more discussion and less idealization. You recognize the new spouse's strengths but also weaknesses and problems. People have realistic expectations about the second marriage and accept its imperfections. There is strong motivation to keep the marriage viable.

It is crucial that you do not feel compelled to marry. Marriage should not account for more than one-third, and preferably one-quarter, of self-esteem. A good marriage facilitates a satisfying life but cannot guarantee it. A bad marriage is more likely to subvert a fulfilling life than a good marriage is to promote it. This is particularly true for women.

Contrary to folklore, it is men who need marriage more than women. Unfortunately, males enjoy their marriages less and value them less. However, on most health and mental health indices married males function much better than single or divorced males. Men report fewer negative effects from marginal marriages than do women. Women enjoy and benefit from healthy marriages but experience more negative impact from dysfunctional or poor marriages.

Remarriage is a choice, not a mandate. You can build self-esteem and have a worthwhile life as a divorced (or widowed) person. Being divorced and responsible for yourself is superior to being stuck in a dysfunctional or abusive marriage (whether a first or second marriage). It is not inherently better to be married than single. Do not marry unless it involves a special person and a special relationship. You are better off choosing to remain single than settling for someone you do not love, respect, or trust. Remaining single is superior to a multi-problem second marriage that you enter because "it's the right thing," "my son needs a father," or "my parents won't be satisfied until I'm remarried." You owe it to yourself to choose well. That might mean remaining single.

Second and subsequent marriages have to be stronger than the first because they face more practical and emotional stresses, a major factor in the high divorce rates for second marriages. Spouses are aware that they do not have to tolerate a bad marriage. They can survive a divorce. Although people want this marriage to work, the divorce rate for second marriages exceeds 60 percent.

A key to a successful second marriage is the willingness to address difficult situations and resolve conflicts. Conflict management is a crucial skill since conflict cannot be avoided no matter how hard you try. Even if you had the perfect bond, you would need to deal with the inevitable stresses and difficulties resulting from the ex-spouse, children, and financial issues. Instead of wishing conflicts were not there, the couple needs to address difficult issues.

Many conflicts can be successfully resolved. More often they can be substantially improved, although not totally alleviated. However, other conflicts must be accepted and coped with. Love cannot conquer all. Some problems and difficult situations are not resolvable. The coping strategy is to prevent the problem from controlling you, utilizing only the necessary emotional energy to manage the problem. A good example is the monthly child support payment that interferes with the finances and lifestyle of your second marriage and family. The flip side is the second family that is disrupted because the payment for educational expenses does not arrive, which causes arguments over how to come up with money and how aggressively to pursue the ex-spouse. These are difficult, complicated issues without easy answers. A healthy guideline is not to sacrifice a fulfilling life or your second marriage over a problem involving the first marriage.

Strengths and Promises of Second Marriages

With these potential stresses and pitfalls, why remarry? You want this marriage to meet needs for intimacy and security. People in healthy marriages have increased self-esteem and life satisfaction. The joy of creating a second life is very special. You share hopes and experiences and build a fulfilling relationship. This marriage provides support for children from the previous marriage. You enjoy the new extended family and are free of the ex-spouse's family.

More than anything, the second marriage provides an intimate friend to share the joys and stresses of life. Being special to and for someone is a primary reward of marriage. A spouse whom you trust is on your side, concerned with your needs, and has your best interest in mind stabilizes and enhances your life. The contrast between this and the first marriage is particularly satisfying. A spouse who provides practical help and emotional support—especially in dealing with children, household, and financial issues—is of great value.

Sharing emotional and sexual intimacy is affirming. Sexuality involves feeling desired and desirous, loving and being loved. Sexuality reinforces your connection and energizes you to deal with the issues and stresses of this marriage and stepfamily.

Valuing your second marriage is crucial. Valuing a spouse and marriage is different than idealizing the partner and thinking of the relationship as perfect. Movies thrive on romantic love: everything turns out perfectly and ends with passion and the promise that intense feelings will never wane. That is a prescription for disaster, or at least profound disappointment.

Mature intimacy involves respecting and loving the spouse for his vulnerabilities and weaknesses as well as strengths and stellar personal characteristics. It means valuing the marriage not as ideal, but having a realistic appreciation of its strengths and joys while accepting its frustrations and problems. Intimacy is less intense than romantic love, but it is genuine, lasting, and nurturing. Romantic love cannot sustain a couple dealing with difficult stepparenting, financial, or household issues. Mature intimacy sustains and supports you in dealing with complex, difficult problems. Being cared about and valued is a special feeling. Marriage is primarily a respectful, trusting relationship. Emotional and sexual intimacy makes the relationship special and strengthens your bond.

Themes in Second Marriages

We respect individual differences and the complexity of people's lives, relationships, situations, and values. Human behavior is complex; there are few simple cause-and-effect relationships and few black-and-white situations. In this book, we present positive, realistic concepts, guidelines, problem-solving and coping strategies, and case studies to help you negotiate these complexities. But ultimately it is your responsibility to decide what is applicable in your life. Accept the reality that a second or subsequent marriage is more complex than a first marriage. Stepfamilies are different from nuclear families. That is not stigmatizing or being pessimistic; it is being realistic. Too many books about divorce, remarriage, and stepparenting overpromise simple, happy, perfect resolutions, like a television sitcom. Life and relationships are more complex, varied, interesting, and challenging. Second marriages and stepfamilies do work, but they are subverted by naive beliefs and perfectionistic standards.

A common occurrence in Barry's practice is a client saying that concepts and exercises are fine, but that their marriage is particularly difficult or their stepfamily exceptionally complex. Barry's response is to acknowledge individuality and complexity and to encourage the couple to individualize the guidelines and techniques so that they work for their personalities, marriage, and situation.

Motivations and intentions are key. Are both people willing to make a "good faith" effort to make this a viable marriage? There is a positive, reciprocal relationship between self-esteem and healthy marriage. Marriage can bring out the best in each individual. A good marriage facilitates personal growth and contentment. Marriage includes the ability to communicate and support each other, constructively express negative feelings and resolve conflicts, experience emotional intimacy and sexual satisfaction, and play with and enjoy each other. No marriage fulfills all these functions perfectly. You need to attend to your marriage and strengthen its vulnerable or problematic parts.

The bond between husband and wife is what gives a stepfamily stability. The tendency is to focus attention on children, finances, or dealing with an ex-spouse. You cannot afford to treat your relationship with benign neglect. If respect, trust, and intimacy are not nurtured, you run the risk of a second divorce or a frustrating, disappointing marriage. You did not get remarried to get divorced again.

Cynicism and negative motivation is a particular "trap" for second marriages. It does no good to replace blind trust in "happy ever after" with cynicism that protects you in case this marriage does not work. Negative motivation seldom results in positive outcomes. It makes no sense to enter into a second marriage unless you believe the bond of respect, trust, and intimacy is viable and will grow.

Dealing With In-Laws and Extended Family

Marriage is a package deal. You marry your spouse, his or her children, and to a lesser extent his or her extended family. However, the package should not include the ex-spouse's family. After a divorce, contact with the ex-spouse's family typically ends, even if you had close relationships with in-laws or nieces and nephews. It is only natural for family members to support and maintain contact with biological relatives. When contact with the ex-in-laws continues, the couple must negotiate a clear agreement so this does not become a source of conflict or stress.

Competition with the ex-spouse is a poisonous dynamic for the second marriage. Even if the comparison is favorable ("you're so much nicer than he"), it is not helpful. The new spouse develops family relationships on his or her own. A marriage that receives genuine support and caring from extended family and friends has a major resource. It is especially important to forge bonds with family members that your current spouse is close to. All extended families have their strengths, problems, and complexities. If possible, develop and nurture supportive relationships.

What if it is not possible or there is a pattern of guilt and blame in the extended family? It is crucial to have a clear view of relationships, rather than pretending everything is fine. All families have problems, embarrassments, and difficult issues. Acknowledge and enjoy what is enjoyable and accept realistic limitations.

Coping With Crisis

In an ideal second marriage, there would be no crises. True or false? Everyone wishes it were true, but it is false. Even the best marriage experiences losses and crises. Common examples include difficult financial situations, a child who does not accept the stepparent, a move to another city causing a child to run away from home, a grandparent who is very judgmental and removes you from the will, compounding stresses that result in a depression, a sexual relationship that is the Achilles heel of this marriage, continuing litigation with the ex-spouse.

There are problems that could be avoided with good planning and decision-making, but some problems are inevitable. Address issues before they become crises. If a crisis cannot be avoided, deal with it swiftly. Hopefully, this can be successfully resolved. Sometimes the goal is to survive the crisis and learn from it so it is not repeated. Some crises turn into chronic problems, which is the saddest scenario. The coping strategy is to stop the chronic problem from controlling your life and marriage. Accept the problem as a sad truth and try to ensure it does not become worse or controlling. One of our favorite adages is that "there might not be a good resolution, but there are always positive alternatives."

Goals and Themes of This Book

This book has three goals: first, to identify potential problem areas; second, to make a plan for addressing problems and managing conflict; third, to help you commit to working together to maintain a strong and healthy marriage. In addition, we have two themes. The first is to encourage you to view the divorce as a sign of personal strength, not failure, and realize you have value as a person. An integral element of self-esteem is acknowledgment that you have learned about yourself and relationships and can make healthy choices and good decisions. One of the most important is whether to remarry. The second theme involves second marriages and stepfamilies. The choice to remarry needs to be well-thought-out and approached in a realistic manner as a challenge that you can meet. Second marriages can be successful and rewarding, and you deserve for that to be true for you.

We want this book to provide you with the understanding and resources needed to assess and change attitudes, behavior, and feelings and help you build a second marriage and stepfamily that bring out the best in you as individuals and as a couple.

CHAPTER 2

The Courage to Divorce

Divorce is not a sign of personal failure; it is a sign of personal courage. It is painful to face the reality that a marriage you hoped would be happy and permanent has insurmountable problems. It takes courage to act on that painful fact. In this chapter, we will take a look at accepting your divorce, adjusting to being single again, and considering remarriage.

Divorce is not easy. Legally, practically, and emotionally it is a difficult, taxing, exhausting process. Getting divorced is much more difficult than getting married—requiring more time, planning, and money. People who deride divorce as a "cop-out" do not understand what is involved. Divorce is a process, not a single event. It takes most people 1 to 3 years to make the emotional and practical transition to being single again. The process is intensified and elongated when there is litigation and conflict over finances or child custody.

Our culture is pro-marriage, especially romantic love marital matches. The culture is so enchanted by romantic love that it encourages people to marry the wrong person for the wrong reasons (a major cause of the high divorce rate). Romantic love is not a good reason to marry. The core of marriage is a respectful, trusting relationship that includes emotional and sexual intimacy. Choosing to share your life is a serious commitment that involves understanding and accepting the person, along with his or her history and values, strengths and weaknesses, hopes and fears. We are not in favor of the arranged marriage model of traditional cultures, although in truth it is a more rational model than the modern American "as-long-as-we-love-each-other-nothing-else-matters" model.

The key to successful marital choice is:

1. Discussing life plans and the importance of marriage to ensure you have shared understandings and values.
2. Feeling genuine emotional and sexual attraction that will evolve into mature intimacy.
3. Discussing sensitive and difficult issues so you develop realistic individual and couple goals.

If people followed these guidelines, the divorce rate could be cut in half. They are even more important for a second (or subsequent) marriage.

Accepting Divorce

A healthy trend in American culture involved reducing the legal barriers and stigma of divorce. Traditionally, divorce had been viewed as a failure. When adult children divorced, parents wondered what they had done wrong. Religious and community pressure kept marriages together no matter how poor the match or how negative the consequences for adults and children. People felt caught between a destructive marriage and the censure and condemnation of extended family, religion, and community. Legally, divorce was an expensive chess game in which the goal was to determine fault and exact retribution.

Do these changes mean that the United States has become pro-divorce? No. Divorce is not viewed as a positive, but as an alternative to a flawed marriage. Divorce is accepted, not promoted or advocated.

The majority of people reading this book have divorced, are in the midst of a divorce, or are considering marriage to someone who is divorced. You cannot afford to be influenced by the stigma of divorce. A prime component of a stable life is the ability to accept and deal with reality. You are divorced; do not pretend, rationalize, apologize, or feel stigmatized because of it. No matter what your religion, parents, extended family, or community feel about divorce as an abstract concept, the concrete reality is that you are divorced. Accepting divorce as a sad fact promotes psychological well-being. Feeling caught in the guilt trap of "why did I get divorced" or "if only I hadn't divorced" subverts current and future well-being.

If you initiated the divorce (in 75 percent of cases the woman does), it is easier to see divorce as a courageous choice. Accept responsibility for your decision and feel pride about ending a destructive chapter of your life. It is harder for the spouse who was left and much harder for the person who tried to save the marriage. In retrospect, most people recognize that the marriage was not viable and that divorce was the healthy solution. Those who still regret or are angry about the divorce are counseled to accept the reality. Although you wish it were different, the marriage is over. Accept this and move on to the next chapter of your life.

Our culture tolerates divorce but does not value it. In the 1960s and 1970s divorce was held in higher esteem. "No-fault" divorce laws were introduced to make it an easier legal process and less psychologically bruising. The hope was that with a lessened need to establish legal blame and attack the spouse divorce would cause less distress. Divorce would free people to lead happier, more productive lives. Children would benefit because they would not grow up in an angry, alienated home. Staying together for the sake of the children or security was ridiculed. In theory, divorced people would be better co-parents.

The data examining the aftermath of divorce have been more negative than hoped. Even with better laws and lessened stigma, divorce is a difficult, draining process for all concerned. The great majority of adults are glad they divorced and would divorce again in similar circumstances. However, they were surprised by the length and extent of the practical and emotional turmoil. People likened it to a "crazy time," especially the emotional roller coaster of mixed feelings.

Divorce and Children

The effects on children are more problematic than for adults. Children want and need stability and predictability in their homes and from their parents. Divorce interferes with that necessity. Divorce affects the economic well-being of children, sometimes in a drastic manner. This is especially true if the mother does not work or works in a low-paying job or the father does not contribute child support. Adjusting to a stepparent and stepfamily can be difficult. If the second marriage is unsuccessful, it means more disruption for children. There are issues of divided loyalty—how close should the child be to the stepparent? Are the children's needs ignored in the tumult over the parents' lives? Does the child learn to manipulate to get his way? Although there is less stigma to a "broken home," the divorce is used by teachers, counselors, and neighbors to explain or excuse the child's behavior—often to the child's detriment.

What does this mean? Are fundamentalist ministers and conservative politicians right in saying that we need to return to "traditional family values" and make divorce very difficult? Absolutely not. Divorce is a realistic solution to a marriage with insurmountable problems. Divorce needs to be accepted, or at least tolerated. It is not the easy, problem-free alternative touted in the 1960s and 1970s. Divorce is difficult and emotionally draining, harder on children than adults.

What is valuable is a satisfying, stable marriage and an emotionally cohesive, functional family. The reality is that some marriages are fundamentally flawed, which affects family functioning and the emotional well-being of the children. Divorce is a healthy alternative when the marriage is destructive. Divorce entails heavy practical and emotional costs. At a minimum, people need to accept that reality. Optimally, they should take pride in having the courage to act on this difficult decision and constructively deal with the aftereffects, especially providing nurturing and support to the children.

LOIS

Thirty-one-year-old Lois, who had been separated for 18 months, was to officially divorce in 2 months. Lois found the decision-making and divorce process grueling. Ray, the ex-husband, was angry and uncooperative.

They had been a couple 8 months before marrying and lived together 3 years before separating. Lois was 25 when she met Ray. She had graduated college and spent 3 years being socially active in young professional bars, beach houses, parties, and brunches. Although she loved the excitement of new people and activities, she was tiring of the singles scene. She met Ray on a beach weekend. He had a share in a beach house three blocks from hers. Both loved the beach, but agreed group houses and dance bars were getting old. They were teammates for doubles volleyball and won in their division.

One rainy day they drove to a small town to browse in antique shops. The hidden agenda was to stay at a funky motel and make love. First sex is romantic and special, and Lois was impressed by Ray's self-assurance and intense style of lovemaking. His desire was overwhelming and he ejaculated rapidly. He was open to continued sex play and second intercourse was prolonged and satisfying. He was concerned for Lois' sexual pleasure. Lois thought of herself as a sexually liberated and aware woman (she had received an "A" in the college human sexuality course). Lois' sexual attraction to Ray propelled and intensified the relationship.

Lois was 14 when her parents divorced. During adolescence she made fun of them and vowed she would be smart enough to marry the right person. Her mother pushed them into family counseling, an experience Lois truly hated. Adolescents need to be motivated to benefit from therapy. Negative adolescent experiences with family counseling or individual therapy often turn the person off to therapy as an adult. The only helpful information Lois remembers from counseling was that children of divorce marry young (under 21), which is a major cause of divorce.

Lois was clearer about what she did not want in life and marriage than what she wanted. During arguments, Ray accused her of being cynical and critical. Lois hated the traditional role of the timid, trusting, dependent woman. She saw this as her mother's downfall, and vowed not to repeat that pattern in her life.

Lois and Ray arranged and paid for their wedding, an informal event with friends and family. Lois had not asked anyone for feedback about Ray. After they separated, Lois' closest female friend said she had never been comfortable with him. "Ray is a guy to play with, but not to share a life with." When conflicts occurred or there were hard times (during the first year Lois developed a severe infection that lasted 5 months and Ray was laid off and was unable to find a new job for 3 months), stress overwhelmed the marital bond. Lois was an independent person, but needed emotional support, especially during the illness. Ray was not there for her. He was supposed to pick her up at 5:00 P.M. after a difficult diagnostic test and never appeared. At 6:30 Lois called a friend, who brought her home and stayed until 8:15 when Ray called from the hospital angrily asking where she was. Lois hoped this was a miscommunication, but realized it was a pattern. Ray enjoyed the good times but was not reliable or trustworthy during difficult times.

Sexual problems are a major cause of divorce, especially early in the marriage. The three most common sexual problems are: sexual dysfunction, an affair, and fertility issues (either an unwanted pregnancy or infertility). Lois and Ray experienced all three. Ray's premature ejaculation did not improve with time, as Lois naïvely hoped. When she expressed frustration (it would have been better had she viewed it as a couple problem and suggest they work on it together), Ray became angry. He used her dissatisfaction as an excuse to have "fun affairs." When confronted, he blamed the affairs on Lois for driving him away. After a reconciliation, they tried to conceive (this is against the recommendation of marital therapists, who believe pregnancy should be an affirmation of the viability of a marriage, not a means to rescue a marriage in trouble). When she did not get pregnant after 6 months, she consulted a gynecologist, who recommended that Ray submit a sperm sample. Ray adamantly refused, saying it was Lois who wanted a baby and not to involve him.

Ray's reaction shocked Lois into taking a hard look at the state of the marriage. In small and large ways Lois felt alienated. Her desire to stay married and have a baby had overwhelmed her good sense. Her respect and trust in Ray had eroded over the past year and a half, but she had ignored it, focusing her hopes on reigniting their sexual relationship and becoming pregnant. She slowly was coming to the realization that sex and a baby cannot rebuild respect and trust, or save a marriage.

Lois did not want to act impulsively. She discussed concerns about the marriage with her best friend. Lois surprised herself by turning to her mother, and was even more surprised by the counsel she received. Her mother told Lois that she would survive a divorce and strongly advised her not to have a baby unless she was sure the marriage was viable. Being divorced is difficult, but divorce with a child multiplies the stress. She gave Lois the criterion she had used when she divorced: "If Ray died, would you be relieved or devastated?" Lois did not wish Ray dead, but realized she would be relieved.

Lois arranged an appointment with a psychologist who did individual and couple therapy. This took courage, given her negative experience with therapy as an adolescent. However, good judgment prevailed. The therapist suggested that the initial consultation include Ray, but he adamantly refused. Lois found therapy a difficult, challenging process of examining herself, her goals and values, and the state of the marriage. Ray agreed to attend one conjoint session in which he blamed all the problems on Lois and maintained a wall of anger and defensiveness. Lois was jolted by how unreachable Ray was and how little she felt for him.

Lois suggested they seek mediation and a no-fault divorce. Instead, Ray hired a lawyer even though there was little to divide or fight over. Divorce is psychologically draining, even in situations where it is obviously the right choice. Lois had to deal with ambivalence about whether this was the right decision, including Ray's vehement assertion that it was all her fault.

Lois found it strange to be the one who initiated the divorce. She had disliked her mother's role of being the helpless victim of her father's decision to leave for another woman. But she also disliked her role of deciding that this was not a viable marriage. A positive side effect was Lois' renewed relationship with her mother. Lois' respect for her increased, and her mother's emotional support was invaluable. She did not judge Lois or blame her for the divorce. Rather, she encouraged Lois to deal with issues through therapy and learn to act in her best interest.

Lois was not interested in a serious relationship or in returning to the dating game. She needed to get through the divorce, reestablish herself as a single-again woman, reconnect with friends, get her financial affairs in order, and organize the apartment she shared with a female friend. She called a divorced male she had worked with and got together for tennis. Afterwards, she explored whether he was open to a "sexual friendship." Lois was looking for a compatible lover to do things with, not a substitute for Ray or a serious relationship. Both realized it would be time-limited since he was leaving the state to begin a job in 7 months. Lois wanted to rebuild her confidence and enjoy a sexual relationship. This helped overcome ambivalence about the divorce and allowed her to be optimistic about future relationships. Lois realized her mother was right; not only would she survive, but she would emerge from the divorce a stronger person.

Complicated Divorces

Next to the death of a child, divorce is one of the most stressful, disruptive life experiences. The more the couple hoped for the marriage, the harder the divorce. The more they had a shared life—children, house, friends, extended family, activities—the more complicated and painful the breaking-apart process.

On the other extreme is the amicable, friendly divorce. Barry recalls seeing a couple who had been married for 5 years. The biggest complaint was that they had a dull relationship. First therapy sessions present challenges in getting to know the people and trying to understand the problem. With this couple, there was little to say after 20 minutes. To provoke an in-depth exploration, Barry asked what they valued about each other and the marriage. What kept them together? There was an awkward 5-minute silence before the man said, "There really isn't anything." The woman agreed and suggested they get a divorce. In the next 20 minutes they negotiated the whole divorce process in front of a shocked Barry. He suggested they not act impulsively, and cautioned them to consider the move carefully and schedule another session. At the next session they were animated and reported they had completed a separation agreement and made arrangements to separate at the end of the month. The separation was amicable, and both were sure it was the right decision. There was no ambivalence or animosity.

This brief case vignette represents an extreme example of a couple who had a hollow marriage, making divorce an easy decision that involved no strong emotions. For 85 percent of couples, the opposite is true. There were hopes, expectations, shared lives. When the separation occurs there are strong emotions and ambivalence. Most divorces are complicated, both practically and emotionally. When there are no children or a house, the splitting-up process is easier, but people argue about cars, money, pets, possessions, wedding gifts and, most of all, feelings of rejection.

Parenting and financial issues keep the couple connected after the divorce and are an ongoing source of stress. Emotional issues cause the most grief. Feelings of betrayal, rejection, and anger predominate. Hurt is the basic emotion, anger the secondary emotion. The person with whom you hoped to share a loving, stable life has become your worst critic and enemy. Why did the marriage end and whose fault was it? Charges and countercharges are exchanged. Who was abusive and who was abused? Who was crazy and who was alcoholic? Who was afraid of commitment? Who abandoned whom? Whose family of origin was most pathological?

Seldom do ex-spouses deal well with each other. The goal of divorce therapy is to stop the cycle of sabotaging each other's lives and focus on respectful, cooperative parenting. The guideline is to avoid becoming involved in the personal, emotional, romantic, or sexual life of the ex-spouse. These are emotionally loaded issues, presenting great risk of comparisons and put-downs (even if not intended). You are no longer a couple; thus, it makes no sense to make comparisons. The ideal is to wish the ex-spouse well, keep clear personal boundaries, and focus on building a satisfying life for yourself.

One of the most frustrating situations is when the ex-spouse plays a larger role than when you were married. For example, the ex-spouse buys a townhouse two blocks away and spends more time calling or coming over than when you were married. Or the ex-spouse insists he be involved in each and every educational, health, or even small financial decision involving the children. Perhaps the most irritating of all is the ex-spouse who wants to give you "friendly advice" about your emotional life or relationships.

Some ex-spouses cling, but more engage in vindictive anger and, in extreme cases, threats and stalking. The guideline of ignoring and not overreacting does not work in the latter situation. You need to spell out clearly in writing what is unacceptable behavior (often with the help of a lawyer) and what the legal contingency will be if the ex-spouse violates these boundaries. This cannot be a hollow threat; it must be followed through. Does that mean the ex-spouse will stop his inappropriate actions? Maybe, but not certainly. In persistent cases, working with a lawyer, the police, and a judge is necessary. Such a high-risk situation requires a well-thought-out response. What happens too often is a series of emotional reactions, little follow-through, and escalating crises. This makes the situation volatile, unpredictable, and dangerous.

The reason you chose to divorce was to make the ex-spouse less a part of your life. The ex-spouse's power should lessen, with his opinion mattering little. You need feedback from people you respect and trust. This does not include the ex-spouse.

NICK

Nick was the first person in his family to be divorced. His parents and siblings had urged him to remain married "for the sake of the children." Nick married at 22 when both he and his spouse graduated from college. Ten months later their first daughter was born, followed by the second daughter 18 months later, after which Nick had a vasectomy.

Nick felt life was progressing as expected until 5 years into the marriage. He received a panicked phone call that his wife, Victoria, was having an affair with the neighbor. Nick was shocked and disbelieving. Their children played with the neighbor's children. Nick was hurt and angry, but expressed only anger. Couples can and do recover from affairs, but the attack-counterattack reaction added to alienation. Friends and family took sides. Everything was couched in "good guy-bad guy" terms fraught with threats and counter-threats.

Nick demanded a full apology. He moved out, and she moved out. The children stayed with their grandparents. It was a chaotic few months, with hopes of reconciliation punctured by angry, tearful fights. Nick felt emotionally out of control. In retrospect, the things he felt and did are hard to believe. Nick compounded his stress by too much drinking, poor sleeping patterns, and impulsive actions. He threw water in Victoria's face; she hurled a dish at him. There were many incidents of name-calling and accusations. At one point, Nick took her car, and Victoria emptied the savings account. Nick had two revenge affairs (one with the neighbor's wife, which lasted two nights). Nick did not conduct himself in a self-respecting manner (nor did his ex-wife). Nick felt badly about the effects on the children. He had viewed himself as a predictable, dependable father. During those months, Nick's parenting was erratic, as he went to extremes in disciplining and then making amends.

The process of separation and divorce was like a roller coaster. Nick and Victoria had three formal reconciliations and numerous informal ones that lasted from 2 days to 4 months. They consulted ministers, doctors, marriage therapists, a sex therapist, attended two couple encounter groups, and one prayer group. The longer a couple is in crisis and the longer the spouses are separated, the more likely the marriage will end in divorce. Nick was feeling alienated but did not want to be the one to give up. Finally, it was Victoria who filed for divorce 2 years and 4 months after the initial crisis. When served with the papers, Nick experienced a range of emotions, but the predominant one was relief. The trauma was over; healing could begin. It was clear divorce was the right decision. When people questioned Nick, he said, "Once a marital bond is broken, it can't be undone." Reactions to the affair broke the bond more than the affair itself.

Nick's biggest lesson was that a marriage cannot rest on its laurels. Nick has every intention of remarrying, but realizes he needs to put more of himself into the relationship. Marriage is not a "done deal." It requires time, energy, and nurturing. Nick remembers his wife saying, "You took me for granted, and stopped caring for me." This did not justify the affair, but Nick realized she was right; he had taken her and the marriage for granted. He will not repeat that mistake in a second marriage.

Nick is the non-custodial parent but is intent on being an active part of his daughters' lives. He did not want to be the stereotypical "fun weekend father." Nick apologized to each child for his lack of attention and extreme outbursts during the separation period. He made it clear they did not cause the divorce and could not change the situation (no matter how well or badly they behaved). Divorce is an adult decision, and although sad, the right one. Nick divorced his wife, not his children. He reassured them that he would be their father forever and would be a predictable nurturer and disciplinarian. He was with them one night a week and every other weekend. He fixed a room for them in his new townhouse. Nick missed daily contact, but fathering remained a priority. He was more conscious and conscientious about fathering than when the family lived together.

Nick planned to remarry and explored reversing the vasectomy. He reorganized his life and self-esteem as a single person. Nick did not put his life on hold until he met the right woman. Being single accorded him the time and freedom to attend training to upgrade professional skills. Nick went to an aerobics class twice a week and joined a hiking club. He became reinvolved in the church and was the chair for a social action project. Nick was prompt with child support payments. Reestablishing a secure financial base was a high priority. Two years after the divorce, Nick had rebuilt self-esteem and felt ready for future challenges and a serious relationship.

Exercise — Reviewing Your Divorce

This exercise asks you to assess your divorce, as it happened and in retrospect. Focus on the positive lessons you have learned about yourself, coping, and relationships, as well as traps to monitor.

Do this exercise alone and then discuss it with a person you respect—your current spouse, best friend, therapist, sibling, or parent. Exercises are most helpful when they are personal, not academic homework. Be specific and active, not abstract or passive. We suggest you think about and then discuss the process of divorce. Then to make this concrete, we urge you to write down the positive and negative lessons from your divorce.

When did you first worry the marriage might end? Was it in reaction to a specific incident, something your partner said or did, a feeling, a concern about yourself or the spouse, a fear, new information? When was the first time divorce was mentioned or threatened? Trace the incidents, thoughts, and feelings that led from ambivalence to a decision to divorce. Was there a specific, traumatic incident that triggered the separation? Was it the ex-spouse's initiative or yours? Did ambivalence, sadness, regret continue or did you know it was the right decision? Were there attempts to reconcile? Did family and friends support you during the divorce or did they try to dissuade or censure you? How did the children react? Were they sad, angry, punishing, relieved, clinging, rejecting?

What were the most stressful aspects of the divorce process? When did you hit bottom? How did you recover? Who and what kind of support was most helpful? Who and what was counterproductive?

In retrospect, what would you have done differently? Were there "blind spots"? Did the divorce have to be as hard as it was? What did you learn about yourself, your ex-spouse, family, friends? What did you learn about the children and parenting? Did you discover personal strengths and skills? What mistakes can you learn from? What vulnerabilities or traps do you need to monitor? Can you accept the divorce, acknowledge you survived, forgive yourself for mistakes made and pain inflicted, and accept yourself as a resilient person?

It is self-defeating to feel guilty or shameful about events surrounding the divorce. A productive, psychologically healthy approach is to focus on specific positive and negative lessons learned. Commit to utilizing these in the present and future.

List positive things you learned about yourself, coping, and relationships. In the next column, write how you can incorporate these into your life, current marriage, and parenting.

Make a second list of negative things you learned about yourself, coping, and relationships. These are "traps" to be aware of and monitor. Detail alternate ways of acting, thinking, and feeling so you do not repeat mistakes. Negative experiences can motivate you to live your life in a respectful, successful manner.

Do Rebound Marriages Work?

A major cause of second divorces is "rebound marriages." The person feels badly about him- or herself and the divorce, and compensates by quickly remarrying (on the rebound). We are in favor of second marriages but adamantly oppose rebound marriages or marrying for deficit or negative motivations. Examples of unhealthy motivations include inability to accept being single, marrying for financial reasons, fear of loneliness, the desire to be rescued, dislike of the dating scene, a need for social approval, pressure from parents or children, pregnancy, pressure from a partner, and falling into marriage as the path of least resistance.

Remarriage is a positive, proactive choice, not a reaction. Marriage is high risk if it is a "back-door, fall-into-it" process. Remarriage should be a "front-door, eyes-open" choice that involves awareness, seriousness, and a well-thought-out decision. You can learn to be comfortable being single again. The choice to not marry or marry at this time should be a viable option.

Many people, especially males, use an affair to leave the marriage. The affair provides companionship, sexual reinforcement, awareness of what is lacking in the marriage, help in managing life, a specific crisis to break up the marriage, and a transition to being single again. Should you marry the person with whom you are having an affair? The crucial factor is whether the bond of respect, trust, and intimacy is viable and will grow. Do you want to share your life with this person? Have you talked out hard issues? Are you committed to life plans and goals? Are there sensitive issues or hidden agendas? Is there a fatal flaw? These need to be carefully examined because the statistics are against you.

The modal (single most common) year to remarry is the first year after divorce (especially for men). The man most often marries the person with whom he was having the affair. These marriages have a high divorce rate. Reasons include idealization of the partner; guilt about not living up to one's promises; children blaming the divorce on the second wife; deciding to marry for less than well-thought-out reasons; finding that this person was a better affair partner than a life partner and experiencing marital sex as less exciting than affair sex; and dealing with a lack of trust regarding future affairs. Are all marriages that develop from affairs doomed? Of course not, but the relationship needs to be particularly strong and well thought out because it has many potential problems.

Remarriage Is a Choice, Not a Mandate

Do you accept being single again, or is it a source of shame and embarrassment? Do you negate your married years? Single people wish they had been married and divorced, feeling they missed something. Being divorced is more socially acceptable than never having married (a self-defeating comparison). We urge you to accept your single-again status and take pride in having the courage to divorce. This facilitates self-esteem and provides motivation for future life choices.

You not only can survive as a single person, you can thrive. Being single is superior to the destructive first marriage or a failed second marriage. You may prefer to be married, but your psychological well-being is predicated on dealing with what is real rather than wishing it were otherwise.

Is remaining single a viable option? For many people it is not only viable, but preferred. Contrary to cultural mythology, women do better being single than men do. Although males put less value on the marriage, they need and benefit more from marriage.

Ideally, people choose an intimate, secure marriage. When one has gone through a divorce, it is clear that a dysfunctional, flawed marriage is stressful and subverts well-being. Being single is acceptable, and for some optimal. Do not put yourself through another destructive marriage.

Does remaining single mean you cut yourself off from people and relationships? On the contrary: an advantage of being single is freedom to choose relationships. This means developing and maintaining relationships with single and couple friends, neighbors, church or community groups, extended family.

One of the psychologically healthiest people we know is a 59-year-old widow (her husband died of an aneurism when she was 32 and she never remarried). She enjoyed raising her son and daughter, having a fulfilling career as a medical technologist, and being an active member of school, religious, and community organizations. After her children were grown, she returned to graduate school and now manages a home health care service. She is an active grandparent, has a variety of friends, devotes time to training and supervising volunteers, travels for seminars and with friends for pleasure. Her life is filled with people and activities. She enjoys the freedom of choosing and not feeling burdened by unwanted obligations. She has had romantic/sexual relationships that lasted from 1 to 10 years. Although she never ruled out remarriage, she vowed not to marry unless she was sure it was a special man and a special relationship. While she wishes this had happened, it did not and she accepts that reality.

You owe it to yourself to develop self-esteem as a single-again person and organize your life (people, activities, family, home, career) in a fulfilling manner. Live in the present, not controlled by the stigma of divorce or thinking of yourself as incomplete without a spouse. Do not put your life on hold until you remarry.

Closing Thoughts

It took courage to divorce. Although it was a painful and draining experience, you did survive. You recognized that the marriage was not viable and had the courage to act on that painful truth. You cannot afford to burden yourself with a sense of stigma or failure. Accept being divorced and commit to a satisfying life as you meet current and future challenges.

CHAPTER 3

Learning From the Past

Marriage is not easy; neither is divorce. You married with the hope this would be your first and only marriage. It was to be "happy ever after." For approximately 40 percent of people this hope became a statistic—a divorce statistic. This does not negate you as a person, especially if you learn from the divorce. The fact this marriage ended does not mean you did not have good experiences or that you did not learn about yourself and relationships. Do not allow the divorce to negate the value of those years, the lessons learned, or yourself.

The most important guideline is to learn from the past. Focus on positive motivations for examining the past. Celebrate and incorporate positive learnings that promote healthy outcomes. Be aware of negative learnings, viewing them as "traps" to monitor so you do not repeat them. The challenge is to learn from mistakes and be an aware, responsible person. Commit to living a healthy, responsible life in the present and future. The trap is feeling guilty, shameful, and beating yourself up. Do not allow past problems to control your life and self-esteem.

Negative motivations of guilt, shame, fear, or anger make it likely that past mistakes will be repeated. Negative motivation causes lowered self-esteem, which leaves you prone to making poor decisions and repeating self-defeating patterns. For example, the woman who feels guilty about an unwanted pregnancy (whether it ended with an abortion, adoption, or keeping the baby) is more likely to have another unwanted pregnancy. The woman who is regretful (but not guilty), committed to using effective birth control, mindful of maintaining positive self-esteem, and accepting of her decision is unlikely to have another unwanted pregnancy.

There are three major sources of learning from the past: your family of origin, dating relationships, and prior marriage. We provide guidelines, exercises, and case examples, but you must truthfully assess and personally utilize these learnings. The traps include feeling deficient or angrily blaming problems on the past. This is a revictimization: you cheat yourself of understandings that can enhance your life.

Does it do any good to berate yourself, your parents or the ex-spouse? It feels good to express anger, but do not confuse that temporary feeling with psychological insight or empowerment. You are entitled to your feelings—sadness, anger, hurt, rejection, ambivalence, abandonment. However, do not let current decisions be controlled by those feelings. Life is meant to be lived in the present, with planning and anticipation of the future, not controlled by feelings and traps of the past. Be aware of past assumptions, attitudes, experiences, patterns, and feelings, but do not let them define who you are.

Family of Origin

How important is your first family—the family of origin—for self-esteem, marriage, and family of creation? Psychoanalytic theorists believe unconscious conflicts, childhood trauma, and unresolved childhood feelings govern self-esteem. They believe partner choice and marital success is strongly influenced, if not controlled, by unconscious factors related to the family of origin. Parents hate to learn their adult children are in psychotherapy because of fear they will be blamed for their children's problems. "Father bashing" and "mother bashing" is prevalent in self-help books and groups. There are groups for Adult Children of Divorce, Adult Children of Alcoholics, and Adult Children of Dysfunctional Families. These groups are helpful in allowing people to recognize that their families were not the idealized "Ozzie and Harriet." The ideal of a loving, cohesive family in which all problems were resolved in the hour allotted is a seductive fantasy, but no one experienced this ideal family. On the other extreme are Adult Child writers, who claim that 97 percent of people grew up in dysfunctional families. It does little good to go from one extreme to the other.

The truth is that most people grew up in families with strengths and weaknesses. Their parents' marriage had positives and problems. The rationale for examining parents' lives and marriage is to increase awareness of positive learnings that can be incorporated in your life and negative learnings that you can monitor so they are not repeated. For example, a common pattern among children of divorce is to marry young and for the wrong reasons (to get away from home or prove they are lovable). Awareness of traps and vulnerabilities can motivate you to make good decisions and life choices.

Develop as clear and objective a picture as possible of your parents, their marriage, and your family of origin. Be aware of attributes and patterns to emulate and problems and traps to monitor.

Premarital and Postmarital Relationships

Assess attitudes, behavior, and feelings about premarital and postmarital relationships. Be aware of positive learnings about yourself, relationships, communication, and sexuality. In reviewing painful, sad, or traumatic relationships, do not be caught in the trap of guilt or stigma. See these as mistakes that you are committed to learn from so they are not repeated.

Extramarital and/or postmarital relationships deserve careful assessment. People feel embarrassed or ashamed because these relationships were secretive or not "right." Rather than be judgmental, focus on understandings and insights. Be especially aware of patterns and themes. For example, one woman realized her relationships lasted between 6 and 12 months before the man turned out to be someone other than she had hoped. She discovered he was married, not divorced; a manager, not the owner; had been married three times, not once; had not graduated from the college he claimed. A man discovered that he clung to relationships a year after he realized they were fatally flawed. He found it hard to say "no." Use insights like these to change the pattern of your relationships.

The Prior Marriage

Carefully assess your prior marriage and ex-spouse. Fifty percent of people remain angry at their ex-spouse 10 years after the divorce. The depth and extent of negative feelings interferes with your life and relationships. You can break this self-defeating cycle by objectively assessing and evaluating learnings from the marriage. Increased awareness helps make your current relationships and life healthier.

No marriage is a total loss. Do not negate the entire time spent because the outcome was divorce. You gained life skills that cannot be taken away. People are afraid that if they admit to good experiences and feelings, they will give their ex-spouse power. You are examining past experiences, not resurrecting old hopes or desires. For example, the ex-spouse might have encouraged his wife to complete her education. She learned to function independently since he was often away fishing or hunting with friends. These were valuable resources and skills, but she wanted nothing to do with the ex-husband's complaints, put-downs, or companions.

One of the worst traps is comparing your life with that of the ex-spouse. Comparisons about money, relationships with children, quality of the second marriage, living arrangements, friends or social activities are self-defeating. The comparison trap is burdensome. Focus on your life and goals. Learning from the past is very different than making comparisons with the ex-spouse.

Surviving the Past and Living in the Present

You are not doomed to repeat the past or be haunted by mistakes and "what ifs." Everyone has ambivalent feelings about the past, especially regarding an ex-spouse. This is reflected in the statistic that one-third of couples have intercourse post-divorce. Feelings of betrayal, anger, and depression are mixed with feelings of caring, attraction, and impulsiveness. Life has few "black and whites."

Life is not meant to be lived in the past or controlled by "what ifs." Accept the reality of the divorce. Acknowledge healthy learnings and painful traps. Examine specific attitudes, behaviors, and feelings; do not settle for meaningless platitudes. The ex-spouse views you, the marriage, and divorce differently. You do not need him or her to validate your perceptions. One reason you chose to divorce was to eliminate the ex-spouse's influence.

JACQUI

Twenty-nine-year-old Jacqui found it hard to believe she was divorced and the custodial parent of a 3-year-old-son. Twenty-nine seemed too young to be divorced. She mistakenly believed, as do many others, that divorce occurs after 10 or more years of marriage. Jacqui separated less than 3 years after marrying, a common pattern. Her husband left 2 months after the baby was born. A common time for a marriage to end is 3 months before or 3 months after the birth of a first child. Jacqui was officially divorced when her son was 18 months old. She accepted herself and the divorce and was looking forward to the next chapter of her life.

Jacqui accomplished this transition with the help of three resources—a therapy group focused on divorce issues, a support group for single mothers with children under five, and her sister, brother-in-law, and friends. She used insights from the past to promote the healing process and empower her to make healthy choices in the present. Jacqui was put off by her friends' "pop psychology" explanations. She was determined to conduct a disciplined, in-depth assessment of her life and divorce. Jacqui enlisted her younger sister and brother-in-law and asked them to be frank rather than agree with or placate her. Jacqui's parents, who divorced when she was 16 (they had three separations previously) were dead, although the stepmother was alive.

Jacqui's oldest sister (with whom she had lost contact) married at 19 as the parents were divorcing. That marriage lasted less than a year and convinced Jacqui not to marry young or marry to get away from home (a common trap for children from divorced families).

Jacqui's parents were a negative marital model, and the divorce was a continuation of their destructive process. The divorce did not stop the deteriorating trend. They fought with as much intensity after the divorce as before, except the milieu changed. They fought about who caused the divorce, child support, visitation, and especially his remarriage. A chief casualty was their ability to parent adolescents and the children's respect for them. It was impossible not to take sides; loyalty struggles and guilt were intense. The girls sided with mother and saw father as a bad guy. They cruelly rejected the stepmother's overtures.

In a twist of fate that often occurs in such families, the stepmother turned out to be an excellent grandparent for Jacqui's son and her sister's children. She did not defend the father or tear down the mother but provided information and a broadened perspective. Jacqui had not known that her father had left the family for 2 years to work overseas, with the goal of making sufficient money to start a business. The overseas venture failed, and he was bitter at his spouse for not supporting him. Each had affairs while living apart, which increased alienation. Blaming and bitterness eroded respect and trust. They continued to be a sexual couple, but there was more anger than intimacy in their lovemaking. They had once loved each other, but were a good example that love is not enough. They failed to deal with hard issues revolving around careers, money, and affairs. These turned love into alienation. Jacqui felt better knowing her parents had had a healthy bond at one time. She never had this with her ex-husband.

Jacqui's younger sister began dating her future husband at 21 and married 4 years later. The sister accepted and forgave herself for the unhealthy relationships she experienced as an adolescent, including one frightening, high-risk partner. Jacqui carried a great deal of shame about her adolescent and young adult relationships. She had hidden this from the ex-husband, and he had hidden a great deal from her. Jacqui had no need to reveal details of her sexual history, but realized the importance of honestly discussing issues and sharing strengths and vulnerabilities with a future partner. In retrospect, Jacqui married the wrong man for the wrong reasons. Realizing it was a fatally flawed marriage made it easier to accept the divorce.

Jacqui acknowledged the strengths developed during the marriage. The chief benefit was her son. Although being a single parent was difficult, she enjoyed being a mother. Jacqui had supportive friends. She had learned a great deal about financial matters and came to enjoy biking and sailing (even though he introduced her to them, she enjoyed these on her own). Jacqui learned to appreciate the advantages of business networks by observing the ex-husband's dealings.

The divorce was painful but contained helpful lessons, especially the importance of being assertive and fighting for her rights. Jacqui consulted a lawyer who was competent and thorough. She steered Jacqui away from emotion-based retribution. The financial and property settlement provided Jacqui with stability and a secure base. She learned to manage her career and finances (she had grown up in a family where finances were not the woman's domain). Jacqui did not respect or trust the ex-husband but avoided the hateful, vengeful trap so many of her friends were stuck in. The emotional support, feedback, and practical advice from the single mothers' group were invaluable resources.

Jacqui was aware of traps to monitor. Chief among these were cynicism and distrust, especially of men. Her brother-in-law was a helpful reminder that trustworthy men existed and that marriage could work. Jacqui had to fight against a wish for a man to rescue her and make everything all right. She dated divorced males, some of whom needed remarriage to make life "normal." She enjoyed dating an interesting man, but realized sharing her life with the man and dealing with his ex-wife, children, and psychological problems would be burdensome. She was open to and eager for remarriage and another child, but it would need to be a special man and a special relationship.

First Exercise—Family of Origin

Be as specific as possible about positive and negative learnings from your family of origin. Writing facilitates personal, concrete learnings. Take three pieces of paper and draw a line down the middle of each. On the right side of the first page, list your mother's attributes that you liked and respected. Be as specific and objective as possible. On the left side, list her weaknesses and problem areas as specifically as you can. People have a tendency to be emotional, global, and subjective. Parents are people first. Be objective about specific strengths, weaknesses, and idiosyncrasies. Be aware of your mother's individuality and complexity.

On the second page, do the same exercise for your father's positive and negative characteristics. What was he like as a person, apart from his role as father and husband? What elements of his personality would you like to emulate and what parts to avoid?

On the third page, do an objective assessment of the strengths and weaknesses of their marriage. People and marriages change over time. Adults whose parents divorced or stayed together unhappily until one spouse died focus only on the end product. Even couples who had bitter divorces acknowledge there were good times and relationship strengths. What positives and negatives did you observe at different stages of the marriage? If the marriage ended in divorce, how did they deal with it and reorganize their lives? What did you learn from observing that process?

If a parent remarried, do this exercise for the second marriage. Highlight aspects of the marriage and stepfamily that you admired. Then pinpoint components you felt were unsuccessful or destructive. What do you need to be aware of in your second marriage and stepfamily?

Share these lists with your spouse or a trusted friend. It is valuable to hear their perceptions of your parents and their marriage, especially if they try to be objective and specific. You do not have to agree—it is your family. But it can broaden your understanding of them as people, of their marriage, and of family dynamics.

Family of Origin and Marriage

It is hard to write about complex, individualistic, and multidimensional phenomena without sounding simplistic. Entire books explore the relationship between family of origin and spouse choice, especially how it can cause an unsuccessful marriage. Family of origin is just one component in the decision of whom to marry. It is a negation of personal responsibility to blame all individual and marital problems on the family of origin.

Not having a positive marital model is a handicap in developing your marital bond. People who grew up in dysfunctional families with poor marriages have to try harder and put more thought, time, and effort into developing a healthy marriage and family of creation. Neither my nor my wife's marital model was a healthy one. We take pride in helping each other monitor traps and creating a marriage and family we value.

People marry the wrong person for the wrong reason (to get away from home, to create what you did not have growing up, to prove something to yourself or a parent). People who marry before 21, especially if the woman is pregnant, run a significantly higher risk of divorcing (more than 75 percent of these marriages end in divorce). One reason people from divorced families have higher rates of divorce is that they marry younger. A prime adage of mental health is that negative motivation seldom promotes positive behavior. As you review lessons from your family of origin, use insights to empower positive relationship decisions.

Second Exercise— Learning From the Prior Marriage

This is an emotionally difficult exercise. The temptation is to refight old battles and justify the divorce. That defeats the purpose and makes this exercise a waste of time and energy. Ex-spouses never agree on what caused the marriage to disintegrate; thus, these discussions quickly degenerate into an attack–counterattack cycle.

Focus on specific positive and negative learnings. This heightens awareness and empowerment. Life and relationship decisions are helped by learning from the past, not feeling ashamed or beating up on yourself for mistakes.

Focus on positive marital learnings. Identify at least three lessons to integrate into this marriage. These could include things you did not have in the first marriage but realize are important. Examples are stating needs clearly, devoting time and energy to keep the marriage vital, maintaining outside interests, keeping contact with friends and family, having at least two shared couple activities, maintaining your sense of autonomy, setting aside time to be sensual and sexual, sharing a common religious or value system, doing "tag-team" parenting rather than competing to be the best parent, sharing financial information, staying committed to not having affairs, going away as a couple at least once a year.

Specify three negative learnings you are committed not to repeat. Examples are refusing to agree to something you cannot live with, lying or covering up for your spouse, isolating yourself and being totally dependent on your spouse, resenting and viewing your spouse as your worst critic, having a major secret or a "double life," punishing and enjoying getting even, being selfish and not caring about your partner's feelings, being so absorbed in career or personal problems that you ignore the marriage, blaming in-laws for problems, coasting and not attending to the marriage, making fun of your spouse, criticizing your spouse's parenting rather than helping with children. Once you have identified the traps, consider how you will monitor them. List the healthy alternatives.

Specify at least three traps regarding your ex-spouse. This is a sensitive, difficult task. You walk a fine line between obsessing/complaining and helpful insights. In therapy, Barry says, "Don't confuse the ex-spouse with the present spouse." Examples include not generalizing anger toward the ex-spouse; realizing physical attraction and romantic love fade so you need to respect and like the spouse; choosing a partner with similar values and interests (giving up the myth that love can bridge any problem); staying away from overbearing, controlling people; not marrying a good friend for whom you have no sexual attraction; realizing you cannot accept a non-ambitious spouse; not letting resentments build and subvert the relationship. Share your lists and thoughts with a close friend, confidante, relative, or your current spouse.

Life and Relationship Decisions

The past is a prologue; it need not control the present. Use past learnings, positive and negative, to empower healthy relationship choices. Rather than feeling guilt, anger, shame, or stigma about your family of origin and/or divorce, take pride in having the wisdom and courage to change your life. Be an aware, responsible person who uses insights and resources to make healthy choices. This is crucial for deciding to remarry, as well as for relationships with children, friends, and family. Self-esteem promotes healthy choices.

You do not need to be remarried in order to have a worthwhile life. Single people feel satisfaction from parenting, work, friendships, family contact, community or political groups, leisure or hobby activities, religious or social involvement, and a life that promotes psychological well-being.

Some people believe marriage is the only way to reorganize their lives and regain self-esteem. We reject this theoretically and clinically. Although it is true that a satisfying marriage is the single major contributor to psychological well-being, marriage should only account for one-quarter of self-esteem. Too often, divorced people feel an internal need and external pressure to remarry. Remarriage is not necessary to prove anything to yourself or anyone else.

Complete the loss/grieving process of divorce before considering remarriage. People who leave a marriage for an affair and then marry the person with whom they had the affair have a high divorce rate. An affair can become a successful marriage, but each person has to assess feelings and motivations carefully. What makes for an exciting affair is not what builds a healthy, viable marriage.

An affair can serve as a bridge for leaving a destructive marriage. For good and bad reasons, the affair is an impetus. Leaving a flawed marriage is very different from establishing a healthy second marriage. The decision to remarry needs to be an up-front choice based on the belief that you can establish and maintain a respectful, trusting, intimate bond. Remarriage is not a payback for being there through the divorce. Second marriages end disastrously as charges and countercharges are hurled about why couples married. This is exacerbated by children blaming the stepparent for breaking up their parents' marriage. Getting married to the person with whom you had an affair raises a number of issues. Each person has to be sure of his/her motivation and commitment.

Closing Thoughts

This chapter asks that you carefully assess learnings from your family of origin, relationships, and prior marriage to empower you to make aware, healthy choices. A crucial component of psychological well-being is the ability to make good relationship choices. Self-esteem as a single-again person is enhanced when you identify mistakes from the past, have a specific plan to monitor traps, and a commitment not to repeat self-defeating patterns. Life is meant to be lived in the present while planning for the future, not controlled by guilt, shame, or stigma from the past. You learned from and survived the divorce. Now focus psychological energy on developing a healthy life and relationship.

CHAPTER 4

Choosing Well

Choosing well does not mean falling madly in love with the perfect person. The cornerstone of a viable second marriage is choosing a partner with whom to build a bond of respect, trust, and intimacy. The trap is wishing for a "perfect spouse" to compensate for the hurt and pain of the first marriage. Second marriages should not be so burdened. Second marriages have their own challenges and stresses; they cannot and should not have to compensate for problems with the ex-spouse or first marriage. Your second marriage stands on its own. This chapter will present guidelines to help you make a wise choice of partner for a second marriage.

The best guideline for choosing well is to acknowledge your autonomy, worth, and self-esteem. Remarriage is an option, not a must. The guideline for first marriages is to be at least 21 and know the person for at least 1 year. The guideline for a second marriage is to be single for at least a year, know the person for at least 1 year, and (especially when children are involved) reach detailed understandings and agreements about money, children, careers, and where and how to live. In first marriages, people are starting out in life. In second marriages, they have to join lives, including being a stepfamily.

There is excitement and challenge in this second chance for an intimate marriage, but each person has to be aware of traps. In first marriages, the common trap is putting the spouse on a pedestal and idealizing the relationship. In second marriages, the common trap is fear and cynicism. You fear this might not work, so you do not invest yourself in the union. Marriage is not about "hedging bets." Marriage involves a commitment to establish a vital, satisfying, stable relationship. Cynicism is an even worse trap than idealizing a spouse. Be aware of the vulnerabilities and problems of your spouse and the relationship but do not allow these to dominate. Marriage is an optimistic statement, a desire to share your life. Cynicism subverts marriage.

Do not marry unless you are confident that respect, trust, and intimacy will remain vital. It makes no sense to marry unless this relationship will be satisfying and stable. Be willing to put in the time and energy to make it so.

Whom Not to Marry

One of the frustrating things in psychology is that it is easier to predict what will fail than what will succeed. The following are guidelines, not hard and fast rules. There are vast individual and couple differences. A marriage that objectively has a 10 percent chance of success can work. For example, a man with a history of physically and verbally abusing prior spouses gets married for the fifth time, choosing a woman who is depressed and has three acting-out adolescents. It would take a great deal of effort and luck for that marriage to succeed, but when it does the couple can take special pride in making it work.

Here are guidelines for people not to marry:

A person who is divorced three or more times.

A person with an alcohol, drug abuse, violence, or intimidation pattern, especially if he or she denies the problem.

A person prone to affairs and/or a person who does not value the trust bond.

A married person who promises he or she will be separating any day.

A person who does not respect or trust you.

A person with a sexual dysfunction or inhibition who promises it will
be cured by marriage.

A person from a different age, educational, racial, religious, or ethnic
background who is not willing to devote the time and energy to
bridge these differences.

A person who cares more for children from the previous marriage or
family of origin than creating a marital bond.

A person with secrets about financial, sexual, legal, or psychological
problems.

A person who wants a marriage of convenience or a father/mother
for the children rather than a genuinely vital marital bond.

These can be overcome, but the prospective spouse has to be
open and honest about the problem and motivated to resolve it
with your support. One partner cannot do it for the other.

Situations You Should Approach With Great Caution

Love is not enough. Problems with the ex-spouse and stepchildren, financial difficulties, and incompatible life goals can defeat
the most loving, romantic couple. You need an honest, realistic
appraisal of your relationship and situation.

These guidelines focus on high-risk marital and family situations:

You want children, but your partner is adamantly opposed (or has
had a vasectomy or tubal ligation).

You are committed to the area; your partner will be transferred out of
state next year.

He wants you to become the primary parent and rescue him from his
adolescent children.

She wants you as an ally to carry out bitter financial and custody
battles with her ex-spouse.

He wants you to make up for his divorce, depression, bankruptcy,
professional failure, rejection, conflicts.

He is looking for a cheerleader, not a spouse.

Religion is important for you and your children, but he is anti-
religious.

You are spontaneous and enjoy shopping, and he is a planner and
saver.
You are expected to take responsibility for your partner's aging parents and/or handicapped sibling.
You are drawn into your partner's legal, financial, or psychological
problems (especially if you were not aware they existed).
Your partner is heavily invested in an activity—skiing, politics, chess
tournaments, astrology, twelve-step program, Christian Science,
mountain climbing, flea markets—that you do not respect or like.

Do couples discuss and successfully negotiate these differences
and potential incompatibilities? Of course. However, these often
result in a fatally flawed marriage. Realistically discuss potentially
difficult situations and problems. Be aware of possible personal and
relationship vulnerabilities. Perhaps the problem can be resolved
or at least made tolerable. Do not marry into a situation you cannot live with. If the problem exists before the marriage, assume it
will exist after the marriage. Seldom does marriage result in the
disappearance of personal problems or difficult situations.

Healthy Marital Choice

The advantage of choosing a marital partner the second time is
that you have a better sense of who you are and what you value.
The single most important factor is respecting the person. This is
more important than physical attraction, shared interests, or her
being a good parent. At its core, marriage is a respectful, trusting
friendship. The person's values, how he relates, how emotionally
available and responsive he is, how he integrates career with personal life are crucial dimensions. Respect does not mean putting
the person on a pedestal; respect her strengths and stellar characteristics as well as weaknesses and idiosyncrasies. Respect is not
blind; it is informed and accepting.

Respect for your spouse enhances self-respect. However, if
his self-regard is based on putting you down, this will be a troubled marriage. For example, if the future spouse's financial abili-
ties make you feel incompetent, this subverts your self-esteem
and ultimately the marital bond. Respecting the spouse is a positive acknowledgment, not a reflection of your deficits. Opposites
might attract, but they often make disrespectful, difficult

marriages. The more central the characteristic, the more important that you complement each other.

Marry someone you trust. It is inevitable that all marriages experience differences and conflicts. Trust means that you know the spouse will not intentionally hurt or undercut you. Even though he is angry, hurt, or disappointed, his intention is positive. Trust makes it possible to deal with difficult feelings and conflicts. If the person's intention is to hurt or undercut as a way of taking control or expressing hostility, do not marry him. Equally important is trusting that the spouse has your best interest in mind and values you. Choose a partner who is trustworthy and values you and the marriage.

Emotional and sexual attraction is a core element in marriage. Emotional and sexual intimacy makes the relationship special and invigorates the couple. Lack of attraction and inhibited sexual desire can be an insurmountable problem. Do not marry your "best pal." Marriage does not increase sexual attraction. Nonsexual marriages are inherently unsound. The person would make a better friend than a spouse.

When sexuality functions well, it contributes vitality and satisfaction to the marriage. Sexuality serves as a shared pleasure, a means to strengthen and deepen intimacy, and a tension reducer to deal with the stresses of life, marriage and stepfamily. When sex is problematic, it is a major drain—robbing the marriage of intimacy. Problems include sexual dysfunction or dissatisfaction, extramarital affairs, or fertility problems. Sexual problems need not doom the marriage. Couples willing to confront the problem and work together to increase sexual satisfaction find that this brings them closer. Extramarital affairs are hard on second marriages. They destroy the trust bond and subvert the marital base. The better the marriage, the more disruptive the affair.

How important is emotional intimacy? Empathic communication is a powerful marital resource. Sharing attitudes, feelings, and perceptions builds a strong bond. Caring and feeling cared about are validating. Emotional intimacy is not limited to serious topics; it involves sharing everyday activities and feelings. Emotional intimacy includes feeling easy and comfortable being together. Sexual intimacy invigorates your marriage; emotional intimacy nurtures it.

Romantic love, the intense energy driven by passion, fades after a year or two. Emotional and sexual intimacy grows and enhances your lives. Be sure the feelings of romantic love can transition to sexual intimacy.

Exercise—Choosing Well

This exercise aims to make personal and concrete the process of choosing whether to remarry and to whom. Being honest is crucial. Do not "fake it." Writing makes this personal and specific, and people are surprised at what they write. It is easy to give flip answers or a socially desirable response. Take this exercise seriously—confront your wants and fears, preferences and turn-offs.

List healthy and unhealthy reasons for remarriage. Be specific; do not pretend or say what is expected. What is true for you? Examples of healthy reasons include wanting to share your life, desire for emotional intimacy, having a trusted friend to share closeness, valuing the security and stability of a loving marriage, wanting an involved stepparent, having a satisfying sexual relationship, being a couple, desiring a house you can afford on two incomes, conceiving a child, enjoying being married. Examples of unhealthy reasons include proving something to yourself, getting back at the ex-spouse, being swept away by romantic love, wanting someone to rescue you emotionally or financially, needing a parent for your children, receiving the approval of parents, desiring to feel "normal" and "socially acceptable," viewing remarriage as a necessary means to rebuild self-esteem.

Positive motivation promotes healthy behavior; negative motivation seldom results in a good outcome. The same behavior motivated positively, such as a desire to share parenting, can turn into a disaster if negatively motivated by a need to have someone discipline or take care of your children. Feeling desperate or lonely is a good argument against remarrying at this time. First build your life and self-esteem.

Be sure you have at least two healthy reasons for remarriage. Find alternative ways to confront and deal with negative motivations. Consider remarriage when your life and self-esteem are on a solid footing.

The second part of this exercise involves an assessment of your prospective spouse. What characteristics do you respect and value? Just as important, what characteristics and problems could subvert the marriage? This is not a matter of absolute right and wrong but of your desires, needs, and preferences. For example, one person would highly value a spouse who desired another child; for someone else this would be an insurmountable difference.

What one respects or sees as negatives are value-laden and individualistic. Make a list of five characteristics you value and five problematic characteristics. Be specific, but do not try to create an "ideal partner." Focus on preferences and turnoffs in areas of health, career, parenting, religion, politics, values, sexuality, finances, friendships, connection to extended family, sports, social activities, problem-solving, drinking, leisure activities, psychological-mindedness, smoking, being goal-directed. This is a matter of personal wants and values, not right–wrong.

Keep these lists. When considering remarriage, share them with your prospective partner. Discuss it not as a true–false test, but how compatible you are and whether you could share your lives. Contrary to the dissimilarities-attract hypothesis, the more people share, the greater likelihood of a successful marriage.

Dealing With Conflicts and Hard Issues

Any relationship will thrive on romantic love and when everything goes well. The reality of marriage, especially a second (or subsequent) marriage, is that the couple needs to be willing to deal with conflict and difficult issues. Choose someone whose approach to conflict resolution you respect and trust. Do not choose a spouse who avoids conflict or demands everything be his or her way. There are diverse styles of dealing with conflict and modes of conflict management. Be sure you and your prospective spouse will be able to deal with differences, conflicts, and hard times.

MARCIE

When Marcie married at 27 she was sure the marriage would be successful and stable. She had taken her father's advice not to marry before she was 25 and was not pregnant (since age 19 she'd been a conscientious birth control user). She married her dream man, with all the characteristics she longed for. He was strong but sensitive; success-oriented but humanistic; wanted two children but preferred to delay until they had a house and money in the bank; had a supportive family who lived 200 miles away; exhibited no significant faults. Her friends were envious and her parents gave their unqualified approval. What could be a problem?

The problem was an area Marcie took for granted—sexuality. She thought of herself as a sexually aware, sophisticated woman who was up-front about feelings and requests. What they had not discussed were his sexual feelings and needs. He enjoyed playing sexual games, which Marcie saw as harmless. She was open to taking the role of the dominant woman and ordering him to do things that pleased her. What was the harm in that?

Six months after her marriage, Marcie discovered that he felt little desire and had trouble getting an erection unless she was dominant. The "games" took on a rigid, ritualistic quality. After 2 years Marcie wanted to become pregnant, but intercourse had declined to less than once a month. Although he said he wanted children, he avoided sex during the high probability week.

He handled their finances. With two incomes, they were saving a substantial amount. He was traveling on business when the phone bill arrived. Marcie casually glanced at it and was shocked to find it was over $600—$420 for 900 numbers. When she called, she found they were sexlines with a dominance–submission theme. Marcie's best friend counseled her not to panic, but to talk with him. Marcie tried to inquire in a non-blaming way but was met by a counterattack of accusations and was called the "sexual police." He stonewalled the issue of 900 numbers and blamed the problems on her sexual hang-ups. She suggested they seek marital therapy, but he said absolutely not and stopped being sexual for the next 3 months.

Marcie no longer received phone bills. She called the phone company and found the bills were being sent to a post office box. She followed him to the post office and confronted him in the parking lot. He was carrying a number of dominance–submission sex magazines. An angry argument ensued. He called her names, including "paranoid" and "frigid," and moved out. She was chagrined to receive phone calls from her in-laws and parents blaming her for the separation. Marcie was willing to try again, but only if he agreed to therapy, which he adamantly refused.

The divorce was difficult and emotionally draining. She discovered things about his financial dealings that caused her to lose respect for him and for herself for being so naïvely trusting. He attacked her character and sexuality. She was filled with embarrassment, anger, and self-doubt. It was a draining marriage and a draining divorce.

Marcie was single again at 34, unsure of herself and her goals. The smartest thing she did was to enter individual psychotherapy. Marcie needed to learn from the divorce and rebuild self-esteem. She carefully assessed what problems were hers, which were his, and what made it a flawed marriage. His accusations and feedback were his way of protecting sexual secrets, but they were crazy-making for her. Rather than attack him to vindicate herself, she disengaged and stopped allowing him power over her. During therapy, she participated in written exercises to identify insights and traps. The exercise about healthy and unhealthy reasons to remarry was particularly painful. Marcie desperately wished to marry and have children but realized the desperateness was problematic. Another unhealthy motivation was to prove she was sexually desirable.

A prime goal was to rebuild self-esteem as a divorced woman. This meant putting renewed energy into friendships, refining career skills, rebuilding family relationships, putting finances in order, and setting up her new townhouse. Marcie joined a hiking club, signed up for a coed baseball team, and enrolled in a continuing education course to upgrade her computer skills.

Within 6 months, Marcie felt her life was on track, and the scars of the divorce were healing. A man from her class was interested. She was acutely aware of the phenomenon of falling in love with the first man she dated. From observing friends, she realized initial relationships were transitional, not worth investing her newly restored self-esteem. Marcie had not been a fan of the dating game in her 20s and did not expect to love it in her 30s. Being single was the reality, and she vowed to make the best of it. A guideline she'd heard from a divorced friend was helpful. "Do not get serious until you've known the man at least 3 months." Marcie wanted to avoid the roller coaster of getting her hopes up each time she met a new man, only to be disillusioned.

Marcie vowed not to marry again unless she met the right person and felt realistically optimistic that this would be a satisfying and stable relationship. Although she wanted remarriage and children, she could have a full life without marriage. This decreased the desperateness and allowed her to view men and relationships in a clearer light.

Thirty-eight-year-old Todd was not a "dream man," but she was emotionally and sexually attracted. Todd had married at 22 when his girlfriend became pregnant and divorced 4 years later. His 16-year-old son was a troubled, underachieving adolescent and a source of angst. Todd owned a small business and joked that his career was his mistress. Marcie liked Todd's upfrontness, his interest in a second marriage and family, the insights he gained through therapy, his desire to live a balanced life, and their shared interest in hiking and the outdoors. She respected his financial expertise, close contact with extended family, and how well-read he was. Todd was someone she could count on and trust.

Marcie and Todd discussed sharing their lives. Sexuality was a loving, energizing component. Marcie wanted a commitment to having children and made sure there were no sexual secrets. Todd wanted her commitment to be emotionally and sexually faithful and an equitable partner in sharing their lives. What Todd wanted that Marcie could not give was to develop a close relationship with his son. Marcie hoped the relationship could improve, but he was a difficult adolescent who had no interest in a stepmother. Remarriage is not about creating miracles and making everything perfect. Marcie realized Todd would not be as laid back about work as she wanted. Their political views were different, and they agreed that neither would lobby the other to change. They visited three churches, and chose one to join.

When Marcie and Todd announced their engagement, they received the support of family and friends. It was a marital choice made for healthy reasons. The tough issues had been discussed, although not totally resolved. There were no secrets. Both were committed to maintaining a vital marital bond.

The Real Person Behind the Romantic Myth

The major reason second marriages are more successful is that you are choosing a real person, not a romantic love ideal. The disappointment, resentment, and anger that sink first marriages are absent. Marrying the person for who she is—with her attractive and difficult qualities—is a solid basis for a stable marriage. Romantic love sells movies, songs, and novels but is a terrible basis for choosing a spouse. Idealizing a person does not enhance love; it results in disappointment and alienation. The person cannot live up to the perfect image. Respect and trust are based on knowledge and acceptance, not hope and myth.

The most important talk between people considering marriage is disclosing problems, fears, and areas of vulnerability. This is the opposite of the traditional "how to find the ideal mate" adages. To be loved and accepted even though you disclose that you flunked out of college, are alienated from a parent, had an affair in the prior marriage, had an abortion, were depressed for 6 months, lost a job because you lied about expertise, abused alcohol, or have had a vasectomy sets the stage for an honest marital bond. Being loved and accepted for who you are, warts and all, is validating. There are no perfect people and no perfect marriages.

You need to respect your spouse for who she is and value your marriage for what it is. The spouse is not Prince Charming; this is not a Hollywood fairy-tale romance. It is a special person you respect and love and a life partnership worth nurturing and preserving. This approach to choosing well will never be turned into a love song or movie, but it promotes satisfying, stable marriages.

ROGER

Roger grew up the youngest of four children and the only male. He remembers thinking how silly it was for his sisters to be so upset with the men they married. Each sister's refrain was that her husband did not talk enough. He felt women blamed men for marital problems. Two of his sisters divorced, although both remarried—one happily while the other had major struggles.

Roger married a woman unlike his sisters. She had a life and career of her own. She did not look to Roger to make her feel important or meet her emotional needs. They moved to another state because of her career. Roger loved the area because it gave him easy access to sailing—his favorite leisure activity.

Roger bragged to friends how different his life and marriage were from that of his family of origin. He and his wife were independent adults, with separate lives and without dependence. He envisioned no problems. A core assumption is that they would not repeat problems they had seen in their parents' and siblings' marriages. They made fun of "old-fashioned marriages."

Roger felt what was wrong with marriage was that it followed a "cookie-cutter" mode. He assumed that since he and his wife did not, they would be fine. What Roger did not realize was that the more your marital agreements differ from tradition, the more you need to think, plan, and talk about how to implement changes. In fact, he and his wife did not put enough time and energy into the communication that was necessary to make their nontraditional relationship viable.

Roger and his wife had an implicit understanding that each could have "fun affairs," but not with someone the spouse knew or with whom an emotional bond could develop. There are two adages about affairs—"affairs are easier to get into than out of" and "affairs can take on a life of their own," especially with time and emotional intensity. Roger fell into the first trap. He had an affair with someone who worked in his client's organization and found it extremely difficult to extricate himself. She called him at home and work. Roger felt overwhelmed by this emotional intensity. At the same time, his wife told him she had fallen in love with a recently divorced neighbor. She felt badly about breaking their agreement, but this affair was an eye-opener about what she was missing. She and Roger had agreed not to have children. Two months later she was pregnant with her lover's baby. This was not the "traditional trap," but nonetheless a devastating one.

Roger spent the entire pregnancy trying to woo her back. The emotional drama and incidents were like a grade "B" movie. Once a marital bond is broken, it is hard to revitalize. To his chagrin, Roger realized the bond had never been as strong as he thought. In retrospect, there had been signs this marriage was in major trouble, but both had denied it. They'd been content to be diverted by jokes and snide comments about traditional marriages.

Roger needed to do an honest self-assessment, and knew he could not do it alone. He consulted a minister, who referred him to an individual therapist. Roger had to stop pretending and confront the pattern of poor adult decisions. He'd been so involved in putting down his family of origin and traditional marriages that he had not taken a hard look at himself or his relationship decisions. Roger had to extricate himself from the destructive affair, accept the harsh reality that his ex-wife hated him and was involved with a new man and baby, and rebuild his life and self-esteem as a divorced person. Roger had a powerful need to find a relationship to prove to the ex-wife, sisters, and himself that he was worthwhile. The therapist strongly cautioned against this. It was highly unlikely Roger would choose well at this time.

Roger began the gradual, painstaking task of rebuilding his life. He focused on positive and negative lessons about relationships. He became aware of the traps of spending too much energy on what he did not want, "bullshitting" himself, and avoiding frank, self-disclosing talks. Roger needed to get his life in order. He was 40 pounds overweight, drinking and smoking too much, in trouble at work, and not keeping his commitments. Rather than looking to a woman to take care of him and clean up his messes, he needed to assume responsibility. There were no easy, quick fixes. Roger took pride in changing jobs, joining a stop-smoking group, purchasing membership in a health club, and volunteering for a Habitat for Humanity project. Roger did not look to a woman to rescue or validate him.

The hardest thing was to stop obsessing about the ex-wife and her new family. When Roger played the comparison game, he became depressed and angry. It was an emotionally draining obsession. Roger's therapist suggested that he learn to limit thoughts about the ex-wife by setting aside half an hour each day to sit in the living room with no television, music, reading, or people and do nothing but obsess. If he thought about the ex-wife at any other time, he refocused on something productive and postponed obsessing until the designated time. Roger found that the frequency and intensity of obsessive thinking greatly decreased and he felt back in control of his thoughts and feelings.

After 8 months Roger felt ready to date again but was wary of falling into an unhealthy relationship. He wanted to be responsible and choose well. Roger talked with his best couple friends, who had been a steady support through the marital breakup. He admired their relationship, especially their ability to deal with conflicts and maintain an emotionally intimate marriage. Roger realized how important it was to feel emotionally connected, a major deficit in his prior marriage.

The friends' observation was that Roger became involved too quickly. They suggested he slow down the process. The wife had single and divorced friends she'd be glad to introduce to Roger, but she was afraid whoever was first would be the one he would fall in love with. Roger agreed to the guideline of avoiding romantic talk and/or sexual intercourse until he'd known the woman at least 2 months.

The essence of marriage is a respectful, trusting friendship. Roger viewed women as seductive people who fell in love easily. His priorities were backwards. As a divorced man of 35, Roger was in a better position to make a healthy choice.

Choosing a Special Person

When Barry teaches college students, they are put off by his confrontations with romantic love myths. When he makes these points to adult audiences (whether single, married, divorced or remarried) these concepts are accepted. You do not love your spouse because he is perfect. You do not value your marriage because it is a problem-free, golden relationship. Everyone has complaints about his or her spouse and areas of marital frustration and dissatisfaction. That is normal, not a sign of a flawed marriage.

What is crucial is developing a special bond. Do not compare your marriage to an ideal promulgated by a "pop psych guru" or a televangelist. Cherish a marriage that meets your needs and brings pride and satisfaction. Marriage is a special relationship with a special person.

One of our favorite couples recently experienced the death of the husband after a prolonged illness. He was not the easiest man to live with, especially during the dying process. It was a second marriage for both. Although they had struggles, they genuinely appreciated each other. Before he died he told Barry how much happier he'd been in this marriage. Although his children disliked their stepmother's social views, they appreciated her concern and involvement with the grandchildren. She helped the grandchildren compose a moving poem about their grandfather for the funeral. Although he'd suffered severe financial setbacks during the divorce, she did not blame or castigate him. She had a nicer house, but accepted the necessity of selling her house and moving into his. Her children did not want a stepfather, but they established a cordial adult relationship. When we had coffee with her 2 months after the funeral, she shared both funny and sad stories about their marriage. He was far from a perfect person and husband, but they shared their lives for 16 years. She genuinely missed him.

Emily and I joke about whether knowing what we know about each other's foibles we would choose to marry again. Remaining married is a choice, an affirmation that the person is special and the bond worthwhile. Our not-so-funny joke when the 2 oldest children were adolescents was that we had to stay together because nobody would agree to be their stepparent. We value our marriage. We are aware of personal weaknesses and vulnerabilities and feel special because we are loved and respected in spite of these. We continue to grow. We do not rest on our laurels. We accept problems and deal with them. No marriage or spouse can deliver on all hopes.

Closing Thoughts

You need to choose well in a second marriage because this marriage has to be stronger in order to deal with special stresses and problems. The marital bond is the central relationship in a stepfamily and needs to be strong, cohesive, and flexible. Do not choose a spouse as a reaction to the divorce or as a compensation for the failings of the first marriage. Be sure you are marrying a person whom you respect and trust, and with whom you can share emotional and sexual intimacy. The choice should be an informed one, based on honest discussions of strengths and weaknesses. It is not skewed by naïve, blind faith or by fear and cynicism. Be sure this is someone with whom you can share joys and challenges, as well as conflicts and hard times. You need a solid foundation for your second marriage.

CHAPTER 5

Money and Second Marriage

 F ew divorced people retain naïve assumptions about money and marriage. Struggles over finances continue post-divorce and are a frustrating, emotional drain. Financial problems burden the second marriage. In this chapter, we will examine how to deal with finances yourself and in this marriage.

Sex, money, and children are the most common sources of marital conflict. Money is a particular stressor for second marriages. There is not "one right way" to handle money; it differs depending on circumstances, values, and goals. Realistically assess your financial values and circumstances and then establish clear agreements. Money problems breed disrespect and distrust, which can subvert the most hopeful, loving second marriage.

Traditional rules about money and marriage were sexist, stifling, and wrong. The only advantage was that they were simple. Everyone understood the rules. The male was the principal (and often only) income producer and had veto power over expenditures. He gave his wife money for the household and children. They played a cat-and-mouse game wherein he complained that she overspent and she complained he was miserly and did not understand the cost of caring for a house and family. Although he belittled her for lack of financial expertise, he wanted it that way. She complained he did not understand how she managed money but did not want him interfering and had elaborate ways to work around him. It was as if men and women belonged to a different financial species.

The model we advocate is the wife and husband as serious, equitable financial partners. Even if their marriage is organized around traditional roles, both need to be aware of income and expenditures. The couple's money management system must be based on honesty.

Negative Financial Legacy of the First Marriage

Many people feel anger and betrayal regarding financial issues from the divorce. This is true for both the woman and the man. Even couples who are cooperative in parenting have conflict and anger over financial matters.

Divorce causes financial losses. A couple combines their income, buys a house and accumulates possessions. Divorce results in the dissolution of what they have built. In the worst case scenario, there are bitter, protracted legal battles over property, alimony, and child support. This is a major financial and emotional drain. Barry advises consulting a divorce mediator; only lawyers win in divorce litigation. Clients complain that each phone call to the attorney costs $200. Mediation and/or divorce therapy is a bargain in comparison to legal fees.

Even in the most rational, amicable divorce, there are costs to both parties. It is financially difficult to split up a household and create two households. The stress caused by divorce (second only to the death of a child) has a negative effect on the person's job or business. People make financial decisions they regret. They overspend as a way to deal with stress.

Women usually fare worse financially because they earn less and because child support payments are often ignored or not paid in full. Financial problems inordinately affect working class and lower middle class women, whose standard of living drops precipitously. The majority of children in poverty live in a female parent home. Problems are compounded as the woman tries to cope with a job that is neither emotionally nor financially rewarding. She wishes she had completed her education or advanced her career rather than staying home with children. Fighting over child support and/or alimony adds to frustration and antagonism.

Although males fare better financially, they also suffer. Hopes for a home and financial stability are dashed. They have a job and paycheck, but they resent the additional expenses. Especially if the ex-wife initiated the divorce, he resents paying alimony and/or child support. Since she wanted the divorce, she should live with the consequences. He rebels against having to help her financially.

When discussing parenting issues the couple strives to act responsibly and in the best interests of the children. This moderation factor does not operate in financial matters, which involve competition. There is only so much income, and one person winning means one losing. Each makes the argument that the other is being selfish or greedy. It is hard for a mediator, judge, or CPA to suggest an acceptable financial agreement.

Financial stress and resentment are the legacy of divorce. Many divorces include a continuing financial arrangement, meaning that money remains an irritation and frustration. The core of the anger is the divorce agreement. In counseling divorcing couples, Barry suggests the services of a mediator and an accountant. He cautions against being financially self-righteous or using money to undo the emotional pain of divorce. The couple needs to reach a financial agreement that both can live with (although neither will get what he/she feels is deserved). The best financial agreement allows each person to proceed with his/her life and meets the children's needs. Child support is set up so that there is regularity and security.

There are two common financial traps that accompany divorce. The first is to become locked in a struggle to financially destroy the ex-spouse. The second is to get the best deal even if it is unreasonable and cannot be maintained. The emotional costs of the divorce are measured by anger and distrust. The practical effects are disruptive to the finances of the second marriage.

The most helpful guideline for remarried couples is to establish their own financial system and not be controlled by the legacies of the first marriage. Except in unusual circumstances, we advise against being drawn into extensive litigation. Even if you win in court, you often do not win enough to cover lawyer's fees. More important, it is a distraction from establishing your financial independence. You are hurting yourself more than your ex-spouse and are shortchanging your current spouse and family.

Full Financial Disclosure

We strongly encourage honest discussion of your financial situation before entering another marriage. Financial secrets discovered afterward poison the trust bond. Money is a matter of fact, not perception. Hiding financial information has a significant risk of backfiring. Do not confuse your current spouse with your ex-spouse. You married this person because you respect and trust her. You want to share your life, including money. Do not let anger and mistrust from the prior marriage control this marriage.

Typically, couples enter first marriages with fewer financial resources and fewer obligations. Couples enter second marriages with greater financial sophistication—sometimes more financial resources, at other times more financial liabilities. They often have significant financial differences. Some have assets, others major debts. Some receive or pay child support payments. Incomes are often disparate. There is fear that the prospective spouse has a hidden financial agenda. The best way to deal with this is an honest assessment of income, assets, liabilities, and obligations of each person.

Barry recalls a couple who had been married for 3 months. The woman had not revealed that her business was about to declare bankruptcy. The new husband was shocked. Did she marry because he was a salaried employee with a steady income? She was offended, reminding him she earned more money and did not bring the burden of a $600 monthly child support payment. This was a business, not personal, bankruptcy. She expected to return to a high-paying position. She felt he was naïve about small businesses and the cycle of business success and failure.

She exhibited poor judgment by not disclosing the impending business failure. It was particularly difficult because they had not discussed financial understandings and agreements. Did child support payments come from joint funds or his funds? When her income substantially decreased would she borrow from her savings or would his income cover the shortfall? Couples need agreements on handling financial matters when things are normal. Even more important is having agreements of what to do in a crisis.

The most important decision is whether money is shared equally. In our marriage all income and major spending decisions are shared. However, this does not fit all couples and all situations. There are a number of viable financial arrangements. The most common are:

- Money and debts incurred before the marriage are kept separate—with all other income and expenses shared.
- Money for or from child support is kept separate.
- Expenses are shared proportionally to income.
- The children's inheritance is kept separate from joint money.
- Hers-his-ours, each person maintains financial autonomy except for joint expenses, which are shared equally or proportionally.
- Income is shared equally—with any expense above a certain figure ($100–$300) decided jointly and smaller expenditures decided individually.

All income and expenses are joint, but each person has a monthly stipend (between $100 to $500) that does not have to be accounted for.

What is critical is having a clear, mutually acceptable system. It is not set in concrete. There is room for adjustment and negotiation as the financial situation changes. However, this is not done unilaterally. There must be discussion and agreement.

Some financial systems do not work, breeding resentment and distrust. Examples include money used as a threat or club to punish the spouse; money used as leverage to control the spouse's behavior; money given with strings attached; a hidden financial agenda; a spouse being made to feel guilty because of lack of income or spending money on children. Guilt and conflict over money can poison a marriage. Using money as a bribe for sexual behavior (the spouse who "rewards" the partner for oral sex) can destroy both the sexual and financial relationship. Using money as a relationship reward or punishment is destructive.

The Issue of Alimony

Traditionally, alimony was given to the divorced homemaker for a lifetime. This has become uncommon as the focus shifts to each partner attaining financial independence. In most cases, the modern approach to alimony works best. It serves as a temporary support while the ex-spouse develops an independent career and financial life.

Both the woman and man feel cheated by alimony. The woman believes her contribution in helping the couple attain success is undervalued. He has the ability to make substantial income and has taken advantage of her. The male feels she is a leech who will let go of the marriage but demands to hold onto his money. The ideal is splitting the couple's assets from the marriage equally and reorganizing financial lives independent of each other.

Child Support Issues

Child support is entirely different from alimony. You divorce as a couple, but you do not divorce your children. The marriage ended, but parenting does not. Children need more security and caring after a divorce than before, including financial. The divorce was not their fault, and they should not have to pay. The "best interest of the children" includes a stable source of food, shelter, and clothing. The family's standard of living will decrease, but should not be disproportionately taken from children's needs. Children understand that divorce means moving to a smaller house, shopping at less expensive stores, and having less discretionary money for their wants. However, their needs remain a priority. Children are not to be used as financial pawns.

Child visitation should be totally separate from child support. The mother's threat that if her husband does not pay child support he cannot see the children, and the father's contention that if he cannot make decisions about the children he will not pay child support are equally self-defeating and unfair to the children. Children deserve to trust that their parents will act as mature, responsible adults in financial and parenting matters.

If there is a financial crisis, the parents can negotiate a temporary agreement and return to the original child support agreement when the crisis is over. Examples include an unexpected medical expense for the child; the father failing to receive the planned bonus, meaning he cannot make the full child support payment; the repair bill for a leaking roof. If the couple cannot reach an agreement, they should seek the services of an outside mediator—

accountant, minister, financial consultant. We discourage threats of going to court or using lawyers to coerce the ex-spouse (unless all other alternatives fail).

Many read these guidelines and say "how naïve and idealistic." The sad reality is that a significant number of males do not maintain child support payments. Many make no payments at all a year after the divorce. Family courts are swamped with such cases. Reality is more important than our guidelines. If the suggestions given here are not applicable to your situation, examine realistic alternatives. The crucial guideline is to develop a plan that protects the needs of your children, keeps them out of adult financial fights, and does not imperil your second marriage.

MICHAEL AND AMY

Michael and Amy were so typical they regarded themselves as embarrassing stereotypes. They married at the U.S. average age of 27 for men and 25 for women and were divorced after 7 years—the median year for divorce. Their financial situation was also typical. Michael was manager of a computer maintenance company and Amy worked part-time in retail. They had two children, a 4-year-old daughter and a 2-year-old son. Amy initiated the divorce, feeling that Michael was more involved with work, golf, buddies, and TV than the marriage. Michael felt rejected, even though it was an alienated marriage, and his feelings toward Amy were impossible to revitalize. His motivation was anger; he wanted to get back at her for humiliating him. As often happens, family and friends took sides and painted the situation as "good–bad." Michael's brother and friends were vociferous in their condemnation of Amy. Their advice was, "Let the bitch starve."

Amy and the children stayed in the house, but Michael refused to contribute any money. This meant no money for the mortgage, food for the children, or payments for day care. Amy's parents helped financially, but they urged her to sue and get as much money as she could. With this type of support from family and friends, neither Michael nor Amy had need for enemies.

Their neighbor was a labor lawyer who knew of a competent divorce mediator. Although both had talked to attorneys, neither had retained one. The person Michael consulted was nicknamed "the junkyard dog." Michael did not want to deal with such an unsavory character.

The divorce mediator was professionally certified and had a consulting relationship with an attorney and CPA. The first thing he asked was whether there was any hope for a reconciliation. Saying in front of a professional that they were committed to divorce made their decision objective and final. The mediation structure was helpful. Financial forms facilitated an objective assessment of assets and liabilities, sources of income, and detailed records of spending for the 3 months before they separated and the 2 months after. Mediation sessions occurred weekly for 6 weeks, and both Michael and Amy had to do detailed record-gathering and budgeting. They had to make a number of decisions, including whether to sell the house, who would carry health insurance for the children, and how to handle educational expenses and child support payments. Michael and Amy did not have to be friendly, but they did need to establish a financial agreement that would provide for the care of their children and allow each to begin his/her single-again life.

The agreement provided for joint legal custody. Amy was the residential parent, and Michael had liberal visitation rights. She would stay in the house for up to 2 years, and profits from the sale would be evenly split. There would be no alimony, but Michael would pay two-thirds of the tuition for Amy to complete an education program resulting in an associate degree. The children would remain on Michael's health insurance policy. Michael's child support payment was $700 per month, which would be renegotiated every 2 years—with mediation if necessary.

The separation agreement was filed with the court. In 12 months their divorce would be final. Although Amy experienced ambivalence, she realized marriage to Michael would be lukewarm at best. She was excited at the prospect of completing her degree. Although aware of the difficulties of being a single parent, she was a more confident mother as a single parent than when she lived with Michael. Amy struggled financially, but she and the children would survive. Michael found the mediation process of value. He wanted to keep emotional connection with his children, which included being financially responsible. He felt the agreement was fair. Amy could not be frivolous and take financial advantage of him. Michael was motivated to increase his career skills so he would have the money to establish a second life and family.

The problem-solving focus of mediation carried over to implementing financial agreements. Neither used threats. The financial discussions were focused and limited to specific issues. Many of the couples they knew used every financial problem to refight the divorce. Five years later Michael and Amy maintained a distant but amicable relationship limited to parenting issues, with few financial squabbles.

Exercise One—Evaluating the Financial Arrangement With the Ex-Spouse

This exercise assumes that you have agreed on and implemented a financial arrangement with the former spouse. This is not about rehashing the divorce or renegotiating the financial settlement. Focus on current finances. The question we are presenting is this: What is the financial agreement and how well has it been working?

Review the legal documents and make sure you are clear about what is and is not covered. Many people are confused or vague about their legal and financial agreements. Review records for the past 2 years (you can get this data from the checkbook, tax returns, a log book) to determine how well the agreements were implemented. A wife should have her spouse check these figures—both as a double-check and to make certain the information is shared. If a husband has financial obligations from the prior marriage, he should do the same for his finances and his wife can check it.

If there is a discrepancy between the agreement and its implementation, decide what to do. You can show it to the ex-spouse and insist it be remedied, go back to court, or accept that is the harsh reality and base your financial planning on it. The first option is the ideal resolution, which is worth an assertive effort. Setting up a realistic system to implement the divorce agreement is beneficial to the second marriage and stepfamily. For many people accepting the harsh reality is the realistic option. If the ex-spouse does act responsibly and pays his fair share, enjoy the benefit. However, you make a mistake by counting on an irresponsible ex-spouse. You cannot allow the second marriage to be weighed down by the financial struggles and anger caused by the first marriage.

Second Exercise—Financial Planning in This Marriage

This is the more important exercise. You have more control over your own finances. Be honest and realistic in examining the financial component of this marriage. If there is something you do not want to reveal state that. Your spouse will not be pleased but that is better than lying, covering-up, or pretending.

Start with the income part of the ledger. Each person lists all sources of income—regular pay, monthly commissions, child support, money from parents, year-end bonus, interest on accounts. Be comprehensive. Differentiate between guaranteed income and variable income (including child support you cannot count on). Share the lists. Be sure you are not over- or underestimating. Even if this money is in cash or occurs once a year (or even if you do not report it to the IRS), be sure it is in the couple calculations.

The expense component is more difficult, but equally important. Divide this into joint expenses, his expenses, and her expenses. Joint expenses include child-oriented expenses, whether for biological children or stepchildren. Gather data from the checkbook, log book, professional expenses, or a weekly or monthly budget. We encourage you to make and maintain a budget. Being honest about expenses is more difficult than being honest about income. Fixed monthly expenses— rent or mortgage, car payments, taxes, health insurance, child support, children's music, and other lessons—are easy to track. It is harder to be honest and realistic about variable expenses like food, clothing, entertainment, medical, gifts, eating out, hobbies, utility bills, phone bills. It is even harder to plan for big-ticket purchases like a car, furniture, wallpapering the house. An emergency fund, a vacation fund, and a savings fund often get lost in the shuffle.

Why do this exercise? To realistically assess the finances of the marriage and prevent money problems from stressing your marital bond. Almost every couple finds at least one (and usually more) issues that vex them. Problem-solve and regain control of your finances. There is not a perfect resolution, but there are positive alternatives.

We suggest you review your financial situation monthly or bimonthly to be sure agreements stay on track. Every year or two redo this exercise to reach new agreements and set new goals.

Few people enjoy money management. It is not like sex, where positive experiences and feelings are the reward for dealing with issues. With money, there is never enough. Money agreements, staying on a budget, or even saving money do not make you feel good or add pleasure to your life. What money management does is remove a source of stress, worry, and conflict.

When One Spouse Is Chronically Dissatisfied

The relationship is under major pressure when one spouse is chronically financially dissatisfied. Examples include resentment that there is not enough money for children from the second marriage because of college expenses for children from the first marriage; the stepfamily is dependent on child support payments from the ex-husband, but they are late or incomplete; the new house is less comfortable than the house the wife had to sell as part of the divorce settlement; one spouse is unable to keep within budget restraints; one spouse's income is based on commissions that are unpredictable, which upsets the spouse on salary; the couple cannot agree on a budgeting system; one spouse feels put upon because the other does not carry his financial share; the spouse without children resents money spent on stepchildren; one spouse abuses credit cards.

We suggest marital therapy. Explore feelings and perceptions about money, review learnings from your family of origin, improve communication, and strive to understand emotional blocks. Awareness of the family system and how that affects financial issues can be helpful. An alternative is to seek financial counseling from accountants, credit counseling agencies, financial planners, or financial counselors. Alternatively, you can ask a friend or relative who is good at financial management to serve as an informal consultant or mediator. Address financial problems so resentments do not build and subvert the marriage.

Our Self-Disclosure About Financial Problems

All marriages have areas of weakness, including ours. We have a chronic problem of poor financial management. We are better at income production than at controlling expenses and staying on a budget. Sometimes this turns into an acute financial crisis. We always survive, but the pattern of "robbing Peter to pay Paul" is stressful. Barry is the one who frets and worries about money, although he is no better at sticking to a budget than Emily. We utilize the services of an accountant to ensure that our finances do not result in major problems.

We have attempted on numerous occasions to turn this problem around. We have read books and tried different financial management systems. Some techniques have been useful and we continue them. A few years ago we reluctantly accepted that we would not master financial matters. Our goal is to maintain the status quo and ensure that money problems do not get out of control. We joke that if one of our books becomes a bestseller this will be our salvation, but we are sure we would find ways to overspend. We are an example of the adage that "there are no perfect people and no perfect marriages."

Our financial self-disclosure is not meant to negate the guidelines and exercises proposed in this chapter. Barry has successfully used them with divorced individuals and remarried couples. It is an example of things being easy in the book but difficult to implement in reality. A guideline we follow is not to blame each other and to avoid power struggles. We accept joint responsibility for financial problems and cope as best we can.

Pre-Nuptial Agreements

Lawyers, financial advisors, and estate planners are strong supporters of pre-nuptial agreements, especially for couples who have children from prior marriages and when there are large discrepancies in financial status. Psychologists and marriage therapists are wary of pre-nuptial agreements, and many are strongly opposed. If trust is a major component of the marital bond, is not a pre-nuptial agreement a negation of trust? On the other side, people who feel cheated financially wish they had been protected by a pre-nuptial agreement.

We cannot propose rules that are applicable to all couples or situations. The positive role of pre-nuptial agreements is to protect the rights of children and disarm fears that a person will be taken advantage of. Keeping assets out of a new marriage and setting them aside for children from the prior marriage makes sense. For example, a man who remarries at 53 sets aside a percentage of his funds to be used as an inheritance for adult children. Or a 62-year-old widow who remarries writes an agreement that the family house will be inherited by her oldest daughter, and sets aside half the income from her late husband's estate for adult children and grandchildren. These need to be disclosed and discussed with the new spouse. We cannot emphasize enough the corrosive effects of financial secrets.

The guideline we strongly advocate is that money obtained during this marriage belongs to the marriage. That money is split 50–50. This is true whether the marriage lasts 1 year or 50 years.

What about those rare occurrences where marriage involves a financial scam? This is a traumatic, disrespectful experience that results in strong feelings of distrust and resentment. Having been married to someone who tricked and used you financially is painful. Not only is divorce the healthy resolution, but fighting to regain the money is appropriate. However, you cannot let your life and self-esteem be controlled by that manipulation. The financial scam marriage is not the popular image of the "trophy wife manipulating the older millionaire," although these do occur. Financial duplicity involves males who marry wealthy women, women who marry for money and/or U.S. citizenship, and men and women who marry out of a need to be rescued financially because they are out of work, bankrupt, or have credit card debt.

Few divorces are the result of a financial scam or manipulative marriage. People marry not just for romantic love, sexual attraction, or desire for children, but the hope that this marriage will improve the person's life. When the marriage fails and the divorce process begins, anger is at its height. One spouse accuses the other of marrying for money. This occurs in marriages that have lasted for more than 10 years. People argue about children and money; neither spouse wants to lose. Often, the fight is really over whose fault it was that the marriage failed. The tendency is to totally blame the spouse and paint yourself as golden. The truth about most divorces is that there is more than enough blame to go around. Seldom is there a saint or a devil. Blaming and anger center on fighting over assets and child custody.

The guideline is to reach a financial agreement that is as fair as possible and that you can live with. The trap is that financial settlements are not reasonable; when resentments build and agreements are not followed, the ex-couple returns to fighting in the courts. Reach a workable financial settlement so you can move on with your life.

Closing Thoughts

Money is a major source of conflict in second marriages. Finances are not just a matter of accounting and legal issues. Money is a complex, emotionally charged phenomenon. A couple needs to communicate honestly and deal constructively with the complex financial issues that can plague a second marriage. Do not allow financial conflicts from the prior marriage or family of origin to subvert this marriage. Develop a financial management system that you respect and trust and that functions in your situation.

CHAPTER 6

Intimacy and Sexuality

Second marriages are often more sexually satisfying. An open attitude and willingness to share are crucial in developing and maintaining a healthy sexual relationship. However, you need to be aware of special challenges, as well as pitfalls.

When sexuality goes well it plays a positive, integral, but relatively minor role, contributing 15 to 20 percent to marital vitality and satisfaction. However, when sex is dysfunctional, conflictual, or nonexistent, it plays an inordinately powerful 50 to 70 percent role, robbing the marriage of intimate feelings. Sexual problems, especially an affair or a non-sexual relationship, are a major cause of second divorces.

The major functions of marital sex are: 1) a shared pleasure; 2) a means to deepen and reinforce intimacy; 3) a tension-reducer to deal with the stresses of everyday life, marriage, and the stepfamily. Sexuality is more than genitals, intercourse, and orgasm. Sexuality is an affirmation of your attractiveness, desirability, sense of masculinity or femininity. Affectionate clothes-on touching (kissing, hugging, holding hands) is integral to your marital bond. Sensual experiences (whole body massages, shower-ing or bathing together, non-demand pleasuring, cuddling in bed at night or in the morning) nurtures your relationship and serves as a bridge to sexual desire. Playful and erotic touching (seductive dancing, erotic play in the shower, mixing manual and oral stimu-lation) builds sexual desire. Sharing desire, arousal, and orgasm energizes your marital bond. The prescription for satisfying sex is integrating emotional intimacy, non-demand pleasuring, and erotic stimulation. Avoid rigid roles or mechanical sex. The best sex is between two aware people who take responsibility for their sexuality and creatively share feelings, needs, and preferences and are open to erotic scenarios and techniques. The essence of creative sexuality is a trusting relationship in which feelings and requests are shared. The partner's responsivity enhances the spouse's arousal. The "give to get" guideline is integral to a satisfy-ing sexual relationship.

The Importance of Sex in Second Marriages

Is sex really that important? Sexuality plays a more important role in second than first marriages. A vital sexual bond provides special feelings and energy to deal with problems, especially with the step-family and ex-spouse. Sexuality reinforces and deepens feelings of being a loving, committed couple. The most important relation-ship in a stepfamily is the husband–wife bond.

Problems that subvert sex in first marriages—rigid roles, tak-ing sex for granted, lack of intimate communication, tolerating dysfunctional sex, one or both spouses having affairs—are not acceptable in second marriages. Ideally, couples feel permission to play and communicate sexually, especially enhancing pleasure and utilizing erotic scenarios. They make sexual requests, not demands. "Intimate coercion" has no place in marriage. If the spouse feels coerced, she needs to speak out and confront the partner.

A major trap is arguing about "the right way to have sex." Each spouse has a sexual history. If sex has worked well in previ-ous relationships, you want to repeat that pattern. However, the "comparison trap" is deadly. The new spouse is a unique sexual person; do not try to force him or her into the same pattern as the ex-spouse. Be open, explore, and share. It takes a couple 3 to 6 months to develop a sexual style that is comfortable and satisfying.

There is not one right way to be sexual. Develop a sexual style that is comfortable and functional for you. When one spouse has a history of dysfunction or unsatisfying sex, it is even more important to be open and experimental in developing a comfortable, satisfying couple sexual style.

A paradox is that a satisfying sexual relationship contributes to a marriage, but not as much as a problematic sexual relationship detracts from it. Whether the problem is sexual dysfunction, an extra-marital affair, infertility, or sexual dissatisfaction, it has a major impact. Sexual problems are corrosive for the marital bond. They need to be addressed, not treated with benign neglect. Even if the sexual difficulty is not resolved, affection and intimacy can be enhanced. Do not allow sex to subvert your marital bond. Sexuality affirms the second marriage and reinforces special feelings. Energizing the bond and reinforcing intimacy are very important.

GERALD AND DONNA

Gerald and Donna had been a couple for 17 months and had been married for 4 months. It was only within the last 6 months that sex had become a nurturing part of their relationship. During sexually awkward and frustrating times, they did not turn against each other and did not fall into the "guilt–blame" trap. Staying on the same team while dealing with sexual dissatisfaction or dysfunction is crucial for your intimate relationship.

This was a second marriage for both. Gerald had a chronic problem of premature ejaculation. He enjoyed sex and emphasized frequency. At the end of the first marriage, his ex-wife attacked him for being a selfish lover. Her searing comment was, "You have the sophistication of a pimply-faced 17-year-old." In subsequent dating, Gerald asked women what they liked and tried to be a sensitive lover, but was ejaculating even earlier. Previously, lovemaking had been 5 to 10 minutes, with intercourse lasting 1 to 2 minutes. Now lovemaking lasted 20 to 40 minutes but he ejaculated within 20 to 30 seconds of intercourse.

Donna became sexually active at age 18. Her sex was both exciting and disappointing. The first husband had affairs throughout the marriage, and Donna had three affairs, as well. She became pregnant and was not sure whether her husband or boyfriend was the father. When she told her husband about the pregnancy, he was adamant that she have an abortion. This was a hard decision, but Donna realized a baby would not save this marriage. Six months later, they separated. Donna experienced great ambivalence and anguish. Although intellectually she realized it was a fatally flawed marriage, emotionally she hoped the marriage would work and felt rejected and abandoned. She left the marriage with low self-esteem and inhibited sexual desire.

Gerald and Donna met at the wedding of a mutual friend. Weddings are happy, optimistic events, a nice place to start a relationship. A problem with dating is that people feel cynical and tire of investing in new relationships. Gerald was more open to a relationship than Donna. He worried about sexual failure and rejection, but was certain he wanted to remarry. Gerald joked that he was "born to be married." Donna was having a difficult time recovering from the divorce. She ruminated over what was wrong with her and disparagingly told friends, "I must have an unconscious personality flaw." Although friends assured her she was a sweet, worthwhile person, Donna was not convinced.

Some couples impulsively fall into a relationship. Gerald and Donna were on the other end of the continuum, cautious and tentative. Sex is a driving force in heating up a relationship, but with Donna's inhibited desire and Gerald's embarrassment over premature ejaculation, neither initiated. Allowing a relationship to develop slowly rather than be sexually driven can be a healthy choice.

Gerald had two loves in life, soccer and concerts, which he enjoyed sharing with Donna. Donna viewed Gerald as a warm, solid guy, unlike her ex-husband. As interest in Gerald increased, so did Donna's sexual desire.

Gerald read in two male sexuality books that the man should discuss the premature ejaculation problem before having sex. He rehearsed talking about premature ejaculation in a clear way without apologizing. Gerald wanted Donna to know he cared about her and her sexual feelings. Premature ejaculation was not her fault or her problem. Donna was touched by his sincerity and empathized with his discomfort. An advantage of a sexual dysfunction is that it facilitates communicating and working together. You miss out on the romantic, sexually driven phase of courtship, but that will fade within a year or two anyway. Dealing with a sexual problem will either forge a strong bond or overload the relationship and cause it to deteriorate. To guard against the latter, Gerald and Donna agreed to see a sex therapist.

Discussing their sexual backgrounds was an eye-opener. They were sexually motivated and interested people, yet blamed themselves for any problems. The therapist warned Gerald not to fall into the trap of performing for Donna but to see her as his sexual friend who would help him learn ejaculatory control. This was not altruism on Donna's part. She needed to rebuild sexual desire and confidence. Gerald was an integral part of that process.

Would Donna and Gerald remain lovers or could this turn into a second marriage? Sex therapy involves more than sexual dysfunction; it focuses on attitudes, emotions, and intimacy. The therapist cautioned Donna and Gerald not to consider marriage contingent on sexual success or vice-versa. Some sexually functional couples make terrible marital partners. Other couples struggle sexually, but enjoy a satisfying, stable marriage.

Donna and Gerald gradually developed a comfortable, functional sexual relationship. Donna's active role in promoting Gerald's arousal increased her receptivity and responsivity. She particularly enjoyed non-genital and genital pleasuring. Although Donna valued intercourse, she found it easier to be orgasmic with manual stimulation. Gerald learned to slow down the sexual process, especially by touching Donna. The hardest thing was to stop Gerald from apologizing for ejaculating early. Sex need not end at the man's orgasm. Donna enjoyed manual stimulation to orgasm during afterplay, even if she had been orgasmic during foreplay/pleasuring. Gerald began to accept that sex was more than intercourse, and sexual pleasure was more than orgasm.

Ejaculatory control is a gradual process involving awareness, communication, practice, and feedback. They used the "stop-start" technique to increase the time of stimulation and engaged in slow, extended coital thrusting. Donna encouraged Gerald to be pleasure-oriented, not performance-oriented. Donna was pleasantly surprised that urging Gerald caused her to take that advice. Her sexual self-esteem and desire markedly improved.

Couples should not marry for sex; nor should sexual problems sabotage a marriage. Sex should not be a "deal maker" or a "deal breaker." Donna enjoyed their growing intimacy. She was comfortable in the relationship, found Gerald attractive, and trusted him both in and out of bed. Feelings of respect, trust, and intimacy increased. Gerald shared these feelings but was afraid Donna would become dissatisfied, have an affair, and that he would feel devastated. Gerald treated sexuality as his Achilles heel, something that would eventually undermine his life.

The therapist confronted Gerald, telling him that the divorce and sexual humiliation still controlled him. Gerald was not a survivor; he was still thinking and feeling like a victim. If he let fears control his behavior, he would victimize himself by walking away from this relationship. The therapist was not trying to convince Gerald to marry Donna but challenged him not to let sexual fears dominate his thinking and behavior.

Gerald enjoyed intimacy and sexuality. Ejaculatory control continued to improve. Gerald might never feel like a "sexual stud," but that was okay. Sexuality is about nurturing and energizing a relationship, not giving an "A" performance. Positive, realistic expectations facilitated their intimate relationship. Donna and Gerald decided to marry with the realization that sex was a positive, integral component (but only 20 percent) of their relationship.

The Positive Functions of Sexuality

Sex cannot save a marriage or compensate for the sexual pain, anger, or disappointment of the first marriage (or post-marital sexual experiences). A vital sexual bond is a major marriage enhancer. Sex is a shared pleasure, a means to deepen and reinforce intimacy, and a tension reducer to deal with life's stresses. A favorite adage is that "sexuality is a special reservoir."

Sex transcends intercourse and orgasm. The essence of couple sexuality is a special way to connect, involving giving and receiving pleasure-oriented touching. Sexuality includes clothes-on touching—holding hands, kissing, hugs, arms around each other. Sometimes what you really need is a hug, not an orgasm. Sexuality includes non-demand pleasuring—showering together, whole body massage, cuddling before going to sleep, making out on the couch, playful touching on awakening. Be comfortable touching both inside and outside the bedroom, with awareness that not all touching has to lead to intercourse. Affection and sensuality can serve as a bridge to sexual desire, but that is not the main purpose.

Non-demand pleasuring and sensuality have value, reinforcing emotional and physical intimacy.

Our favorite way to think of intercourse is as a special pleasuring technique. Sexuality is a sharing of pleasure, not a performance. Intercourse is an integral part of sexuality, but it's a myth that sex equals intercourse. A common couple struggle involves frequency of sex. What they are really arguing about is intercourse frequency. Intimate couples do not treat sexuality as a power struggle revolving around frequency. They are aware of and value sexual variability and flexibility. If both partners had to be equally desirous, aroused, and orgasmic each time, sex would be a chore, not a pleasure. Commonly, one partner is more desirous and initiates intercourse. Traditionally, this was the male, but in many marriages, it is the woman. Both partners are involved, but it is an unrealistic demand that desire and arousal be equal. Sometimes intercourse involves high desire, high arousal, with both partners orgasmic and sharing emotional satisfaction. If that occurs two to four times a month, the couple can feel lucky. Thinking it should happen each time is silly and self-defeating. The best example of an unrealistic goal is simultaneous orgasm. Most couples never have simultaneous orgasms and, those who do find it nowhere as fulfilling as they had been led to believe.

As with other components of a second marriage, realistic sexual expectations are vital. Sometimes "quickie" intercourse is fine. Sometimes what you need is holding and stroking. At other times, one spouse pleasures the other to orgasm but is not interested in being aroused herself. Sometimes playful touching builds a bridge for sex after the children are in bed. Sexuality can play a number of enhancing roles in marriage.

Avoiding the Comparison Trap

The advantage of both partners being virgins at marriage is that neither has to be afraid of being compared to a previous lover. We are not in favor of re-creating the tradition of virgin marriages (especially not for second marriages).

The comparison trap is poisonous. Each spouse is a unique sexual person with her/his strengths and vulnerabilities. Whether the first marriage and other sexual experiences were marvelous or disastrous is not the point. Each couple is unique, and the partners must develop their own sexual style. Romantic-love couples initially experience strong desire, attraction, and passionate sex. If sexuality is to remain a satisfying part of the marriage, they have to continue sharing sexual feelings and preferences and develop an intimate, interactive couple sexual style.

What is the value of comparing your current spouse with an ex-spouse or others? Truthfully, we have never heard anything positive about doing so. What is valuable is awareness of your sexual feelings and preferences. Sharing those and making requests facilitates a comfortable, satisfying couple sexual style. The comparison game subverts marital sexuality.

Contraception, Conception, and Sterilization

When we listed the functions of sexuality, we purposely left out the one traditionally listed first, conceiving a baby. We are strong believers in planned, wanted children and have devoted an entire chapter (Chapter 8) to the decision of whether to have a baby.

This is one of the most important, yet difficult, decisions because there is no middle ground; you either have a child or you do not. Many people decide by chance. They do not use contraception or use it haphazardly. An unplanned, unwanted pregnancy puts enormous stress on a second marriage. We strongly suggest using effective contraception unless you make a positive decision to conceive. If you decide not to have a baby, we suggest sterilization. Your sexual life is freer when you are not worried about an unwanted pregnancy.

Who should be sterilized? If you consider only medical and cost factors, the man would have a vasectomy. Then why are there more tubal ligations than vasectomies? The person more committed to not having a child is the one who opts to be sterilized. Some men have irrational psychological or sexual fears of vasectomy. Although it is possible to reverse a vasectomy (it is much easier than a tubal ligation), sterilization should be viewed as a permanent decision. The person more comfortable with sterilization and most committed to not having additional children is the one who volunteers.

There is no perfect contraceptive, but there are good alternatives. The most commonly used contraceptives are the birth control pill, injections, condom, diaphragm, and the IUD. The man and woman have to discuss (in consultation with a gynecologist) what they are comfortable with. One factor is that the contraceptive not interfere with sexual pleasure and functioning.

If the partners decide they want a child, trying to get pregnant facilitates sexual desire. Enjoy the opportunity.

Agreements About Extra-Marital Affairs

The issue of extra-marital affairs is particularly sensitive in second marriages. Many, if not most, first marriages involved an affair. That does not mean that the affair caused the divorce. Often the affair reflected a problem in the marriage. Some people use an affair as an impetus to leave the marriage. One function of an affair is to test if he experiences desire and erection with a different partner. Marriages end because the ex-spouse was having an affair and would not give it up.

Almost everyone advocates not having affairs. Yet, affairs take place in many marriages. What does that mean and what kind of understandings and agreements can you develop? It is hard to be rational and objective in reaching explicit agreements about this sensitive topic.

No matter what "pop psychology" books or talk show hosts say, extra-marital sex is not a simple yes–no issue. Extra-marital affairs are complex and variable in their motivation, how the affair occurs, and its effects on the individual and marriage. You can divide affairs into three categories:

1. High-opportunity, low-involvement affair: Characterized by impulsiveness, minimal emotional connection, and may involve payment (massage parlor or prostitute). This is the most common type of male affair.

2. Ongoing, compartmentalized affair: A relationship primarily sexual as opposed to emotion based, enjoyable but not committed, and not a direct threat to the marriage.

3. Comparison affair: This relationship meets significant sexual and/or emotional needs not met by the marriage. It can be a 1-year ongoing love affair with a neighbor or a highly charged 2-week relationship starting at a convention. People leave their marriages for comparison affairs. This is the most common type of female affair.

Each person has different feelings, values, and experiences with affairs. In an ideal scenario (before marriage) the couple would have a frank discussion about the role of marital sexuality, thoughts, and feelings about affairs, and reach an agreement. Unfortunately, this is seldom done. Affairs almost always come up in the context of suspicion, discovery, or a crisis.

The better the marriage, the more reason to decide against an affair. The potential for stress and disruption is great. It is not worth putting a satisfying marriage at risk. Prevention is the most cost-efficient strategy. The best prevention technique is a clear understanding about the type of person and affair each partner is vulnerable to and a strategy to avoid falling into that type of affair. Secrecy provides a breeding ground for affairs. Couples are encouraged to make an agreement that if the spouse is in a high-risk situation, he or she commits to discussing this before acting on it. Affairs thrive on secrecy. This technique ensures that the spouse does not fall into an affair or impulsively acts out.

The issue of extra-marital affairs need not become a "hot," supersensitive topic. Avoid the extremes of denial or obsessive focus. Deal with current feelings and realities; do not be controlled by the past or fears about the future. Affairs can be handled like other issues. The couple reaches an understanding and agreement. The most common is that both people agree not to have affairs. The second most common is that if there is an affair, it be kept totally separate from the marriage. Examples include affairs when the spouse is traveling or an affair with someone living at least 100 miles away. Comparison affairs destroy marriages, and couples vow to avoid them. Affairs are high risk. If you choose to have affairs, keep them away from the marriage, within safe parameters, and protect yourself (and your partner) against sexually transmitted diseases, HIV, and pregnancy.

Exercise—Sharing Sexual Requests and Vulnerabilities

How can you promote healthy marital sexuality? How can you facilitate sexuality as a shared pleasure, a means to strengthen intimacy, and a tension reducer? This exercise has three phases—positive learnings and requests, informing the spouse about vulnerabilities and traps, and engaging in a non-demand pleasuring exercise.

The first phase involves sharing (verbally or in writing) what your conditions are for good sex and making three specific requests to facilitate sexual pleasure. Examples include showering together as a sensual experience; use of a body lotion to enhance stimulation; pleasuring that lasts at least 20 minutes; waiting until both partners are highly aroused before beginning intercourse; being sexual early in the evening when you are awake and aware; switching intercourse positions at least once during lovemaking; kissing before, during and after intercourse; having the woman guide intromission; engaging in oral sex right before intercourse; being sexual in a place other than the bedroom; lying down and talking for 10 minutes after intercourse; "making out" on the sofa without it leading to intercourse; being sexual while watching an erotic video; use of multiple stimulation during intercourse.

Share preferences; these are requests, not demands. Sexuality is about pleasure, not performance, and cooperation, not competition.

The second part of the exercise is to create a list (oral or written) of sexual vulnerabilities or traps to monitor. Be clear and specific about what is uncomfortable or negative. The intention is not to inhibit sexual expression, but to facilitate comfort and awareness. Examples of vulnerabilities/aversive components include not forcing intromission if there is minimal lubrication; aversion to "dirty talk"; dislike of anal stimulation; no erotic or sexual touching in front of children; not demanding sex when drinking; no threats associated with sex; no comparisons with a former spouse or ex-lovers; no bragging about sex in front of friends; not demanding each experience be great; not analyzing a sexual experience immediately afterward; no "intimate coercion"; no sex after a fight; and not using sex to prove something to yourself or anyone else.

Honor these requests and the sexual relationship will grow in comfort and trust. Awareness of vulnerabilities and traps facilitates sexual expression; it does not inhibit healthy sexuality.

The third phase of this exercise involves a non-demand pleasuring experience. Do this in silence so you can focus on feelings and sensations. Afterward, verbally share what you found sensuous and pleasurable. Be aware of what did not feel good and what you want to try next time.

Focus on sensuality; refrain from genital stimulation or intercourse. Giving and receiving pleasurable touching is the bedrock of sexual desire. Set aside 45 minutes to an hour and a half. Put the answering machine on or take the phone off the hook. Be sure the kids are at someone's house or asleep. Lock the door so you are not distracted or interrupted. Traditionally, it is the male's role to initiate. Ideally, both partners feel free to initiate sensual and/or sexual activity. This time let the woman be the initiator.

Begin by sitting and talking over a cup of coffee or glass of wine. Recall an experience when you felt particularly intimate. Touching facilitates closeness. Ask the spouse to put his hands out and explore his hands and fingers. Notice differences in size and texture. How would you feel if this were the last time you were to touch his hands? Caress each hand in a tender, caring manner.

Take a shower or bath together. Feel comfortable with nudity and sensual stimuli. Try a different soap, bubble bath, or experiment with temperature or types of spray. Soap his back, caressing as you do. Trace the muscles and contours, gently rub and massage. Soap his front and touch the hollows of his neck and soft area below the ribs. Soap hips and legs. Let him soap you.

Dry each other slowly and tenderly. Look at your spouse as if this is the first time you have seen him. Notice one or two things you find particularly attractive. Slide his arms around your waist; enjoy the warmth and closeness.

Go to your bedroom nude or put on a robe, leaving it at the door. Pleasuring is best done in the nude. Be sure the room is at a comfortable temperature and there is enough light to see your partner's body. Some couples enjoy doing this by candlelight and use scented candles to offer additional sensual stimuli. Put on your favorite music to add to the ambiance.

The man has three tasks. The first is allow himself to be passive and receive pleasure. The second is keep his eyes closed so he can concentrate on feelings (and make her feel less self-conscious). The third task is to be aware of what parts of his body and types of touch are sensuous.

The woman can provide a wide variety of touch. Touch for yourself rather than trying to second guess what he wants. Look at and stroke from the top of his head to the bottom of his feet. Talk can be distracting; communicate through touch.

Massage his shoulders gently. Do not give a vigorous back rub. Rub tenderly, using your entire hand; move slowly down the back and sides. Allow touching to be gentle and rhythmic; avoid sudden movements. Be aware of appealing characteristics you might not have noticed— freckles, tiny scars, muscle indentations. When you reach the waist, place your thumbs together, spread your fingers, and gently press and knead as you caress his sides and lower back.

The giver provides a variety of touching so the recipient can increase his awareness of sensuality and pleasure. Feel free to innovate. Be spontaneous. These are guidelines, not rigid rules. Hold and caress his feet. Notice the length of his toes, the texture of the nails. Place your palm so it covers the arch, and curl your fingers over the top of his foot. Notice the heel as you rub it with the palm of your hand.

Once you have explored the back of his body, slowly roll him over and start on the front. Touch his face. Kiss his closed eyelids. Gently caress away the lines from his forehead. Stroke his face and be aware of at least one attractive feature. Give a scalp massage or gently run your fingers through his hair. Slowly and tenderly stroke his chest. Tickle chest hairs or play with his nipples; many men enjoy this. Rub your hands around his stomach and ribs. Feel free to look at his penis and testicles, but do not touch. He may or may not have an erection. Women view an erection as pressure or a demand rather than seeing it as a compliment, a natural response to pleasure. Enjoy his penis for what it is, a special part of him. Let the exploration and touching proceed to his inner thighs and legs.

When you have completed this sensuous exploration, switch roles. Most couples switch during the exercise, although some prefer a separate session with the roles reversed. In an intimate relationship both people are comfortable giving and receiving pleasure. However, many males find it harder to receive than give.

The man need not try to emulate the woman's approach. He should touch her in ways he enjoys. Explore, be comfortable, share sensuality. The key is slow, tender, rhythmic, caring touching. Enjoy giving. Traditionally, when a man touches a woman his goal is to "turn her on" and prove he is a good lover. There is no need for either person to prove anything. The woman focuses on the types of touch and areas of her body that feel sensuous. The man can enjoy giving touch and sharing pleasure.

Afterward, or the next day, sit over a cup of coffee or a drink and discuss the experience. Share positive feelings and perceptions. Then discuss negatives with requests for change. What did you learn about initiating and sensuality that you can incorporate into lovemaking? How can you integrate sensuality with eroticism and intercourse? Let affection, sensuality, and eroticism be a flowing part of your marriage.

Closing Thoughts

The primary relationship in a stepfamily is the husband–wife bond. Sexuality can energize the bond, deepening and reinforcing intimacy. A couple that is sexually open and vulnerable generalizes these feelings to other areas of the marriage. Sexuality helps ease the inevitable hassles and stresses of your second marriage and stepfamily. An intimate sexual relationship provides an energized base for the marriage and motivation to deal with difficult issues.

CHAPTER 7

Stepfamilies and Stepparenting—
Yours, Mine and Ours

Stepfamilies are different from nuclear families. Stepparenting books optimistically promise an idyllic family. In truth, stepfamilies are complex and vulnerable to problems. They present special challenges, especially that of coordinating different traditions and the realities of two families. This chapter will help you understand your stepfamily and enhance your confidence as a parent or stepparent.

Rather than trying to sidestep difficulties or wishing it were easy, meet the challenges and make your stepfamily as functional and satisfying as possible. Do not strive for perfection; few stepfamilies are perfect. But then few nuclear families are either.

There are many types of stepfamilies. There are families in which one spouse is the custodial parent of her children and the other spouse is the non-custodial parent of his children; one spouse has a child and the other does not; one spouse has custody of the children and the other spouse shares joint custody; one spouse has children from a first marriage, the other spouse does not and there is a child from this marriage; both spouses have children from previous marriages and children from this marriage. To complicate things further, the ex-spouse might have a stepfamily, meaning the child is dealing with two households and two stepfamilies. In a nuclear family, there is an assumed set of expectations and boundaries. In a stepfamily these expectations and boundaries have to be discussed and established. Stepfamily roles are more flexible and variable. The role of the stepparent makes these families more complex. When two people who have been previously divorced with no children marry and have two children, this family functions as a nuclear family. It is not remarriage per se that causes the complications; the crucial factor is children from a previous marriage or a non-marital relationship.

Challenge, Not a Self-Fulfilling Prophecy

Articles on stepfamilies emphasize problems, pitfalls, and difficulties. This can result in a self-fulfilling prophecy, which is of no benefit to you or your children. In truth, the majority of stepfamilies and children are functional, and some thrive in impressive ways.

Remarried adults can view stepparenting and stepfamilies as a challenge. Being naïvely optimistic and expecting the family to be the "Brady Bunch" does no one any good. Nor does obsessing about problems and making these a self-fulfilling prophecy. Maintain positive, realistic expectations. View issues and problems as a challenge to deal with as successfully as possible.

The Stepparent's Dilemma

The major complaint of stepparents is that they feel like undervalued, second-class citizens. This is common to both stepfathers and stepmothers. The stereotypes of the "wicked stepmother" and the "heavy-handed stepfather" are powerful. The stepparent receives much blame but little credit for good intentions and efforts to care for children and make the family work. Stepparents complain of their ambiguous role. What responsibilities do they have for the child, especially setting rules and discipline? It is easier to say what not to do than what to do. What are the rewards and satisfactions for a stepparent?

The spouse appreciates the stepparent more than the children do. Typically, children view the stepparent as an intruder or take his contributions for granted. Seldom is the stepparent valued. This is especially true of adolescent girls and stepfathers. The younger the child, the more likely he will form a positive bond with a stepparent, especially if it is a full-time custodial situation. Stepfamilies differ depending on whether the child is 5 or 15. Preadolescents and teenagers usually do not form strong bonds with stepparents; if you are an exception consider yourself very lucky.

A suggestion is to establish at least one activity with the child that is positive for the stepparent. For example, a stepmother might have a difficult relationship with an 11-year-old stepson but does share a love of horses and riding, which serves as a "port in the storm" in their tumultuous relationship. A stepfather coaches his stepdaughter's soccer team both because he enjoys coaching and because it is a positive connection for them. A stepmother enjoys helping her 9-year-old stepson write a school report when he is with them every other weekend. The shared activity can be productive or fun. But stepparents need reinforcement for their difficult role.

What is the best way to deal with the hard times of being a stepparent, especially the taunt, "I don't have to, you're not my father"? The sensible guidance, although hard to follow, is do not fall for it. Adults lose "yes-you-will" power struggles. Remember, you are the adult with better emotional control and problem-solving skills. Children want the stepparent to lose control, so they can justify being alienated and feeling victimized. Stepparents want what biological parents want: to love and feel loved by the child, to see the child develop in a healthy manner, to enjoy the child and parenting, to set rules and discipline. It is not unreasonable to want this, but it is difficult to achieve. Few stepparents find as much satisfaction from parenting as do biological parents. That is a harsh, but true, reality.

The stepparent should not try to replace the biological parent. The marriage is over, not the parenting relationship. Even if the biological parent totally drops out of the child's life, the stepparent does not become the primary parent (unless the child is quite young). A reasonable expectation is establishing "a favorite uncle" relationship. You have a crucial, positive role in the child's development; this role includes guidance, communication, affection, discipline, and monitoring behavior and school work. You are not in a loyalty competition with the biological parent; nor are you competing with the ex-spouse. This guideline is even more important with preadolescent or adolescent children, who are not looking for a parent-substitute. They do not want someone to take over as primary parent, and especially not as disciplinarian.

Traps to Avoid

The worst trap is the "good–bad" power struggle. "My kids are good; your kids are bad"; "You don't treat my kids well, so why should I treat your kids well"; "If you don't love my kids, you don't love me"; "Everything was fine until you arrived—you've wrecked the family"; "You have a choice: either the kids go or I do." A power struggle means you are fighting so hard against something that you have forgotten what the original positive goal was. Remember, the husband–wife bond is the core relationship in a stepfamily. Do not put it at risk by a power struggle over children and parenting.

Each child has strengths and weaknesses. Each biological parent has strengths and weaknesses. Each stepparent has strengths and weaknesses. Each stepfamily has strengths and weaknesses. If you keep that in mind and try to understand, communicate, and problem-solve, it is easier to stay out of the power struggle.

Childhood and adolescence are a series of developmental processes, not crises. A common trap is confusing normal problems with true crises. The child having a bad year in school, the adolescent who begins smoking, the child angry at the biological parent and turning to the stepparent—these are common difficulties. Serious troubles and genuine emergencies do occur, but reacting to every difficulty as a disaster is self-defeating and draining. In areas of genuine crisis or for chronic problems, we advise seeking professional assistance (Appendix A has suggestions for choosing a family therapist).

Another trap is blaming all problems on the divorce. Using divorce as an excuse for every childhood or parenting problem is also self-defeating. Children in stepfamilies can and do thrive—emotionally, academically, and psychologically. Learning to be independent, flexible, able to deal with multiple relationships, and gaining increased empathy and awareness are advantages of growing up in a stepfamily. You take less for granted and are more perceptive and responsible.

Apologizing for yourself or your family is not healthy. Feeling guilty or shameful about the divorce or stepfamily does nothing for you or the children. Trying to win others over or change their judgment is a waste of energy that could be better spent on improving self-esteem and family relationships. When you feel accepting, others will respond. Those who remain judgmental have their own issues.

The Living-Together Family

What about the non-married couple and family? Marriage is a commitment to share your lives with the intention of permanence. Some people marry because it is the "right thing," only to regret that decision. The "living-together" family may or may not be permanent. This is a decision for adults, not children. Children should not have to go through the emotional roller coaster of wondering whether the adults will marry and this family will be permanent.

The biological parent is responsible for the children. The partner's role with the children should be clear but should not include promises of security. Even though a good relationship is established between the woman and 9-year-old, if the couple breaks up she will not have a role in the boy's life. A major guideline is "don't make promises you can't keep." Children are very attuned to feelings of betrayal and broken trust. Children cannot save a relationship; nor should they have the power to subvert a relationship.

The question is does this family work? Part of making a second marriage and stepfamily functional is the commitment and willingness to put time and energy into ensuring its viability. Some couples discover when living together that the differences are so great that love and trying are not enough. Barry remembers a couple who cared a great deal and had a strong sexual attraction but found after living together for 5 months that differences in financial matters, political incompatibility, parental values, and dramatically different preferences about organizing a household doomed the relationship. They were an excellent dating couple, but theirs would be a nonviable, dysfunctional marriage. Love is not enough and neither are good intentions. Good intentions are necessary but not sufficient for a successful marriage and stepfamily.

We strongly advise against a partner assuming a stepparent role until the couple is married or committed to being married. Being a stepparent signifies a commitment to stability; the assumption is that the marriage will endure and so will the stepparent relationship. There are no ironclad guarantees in life, but this is a reasonable assumption.

The stigma of being a non-married couple is less powerful than it used to be, but the uncertainties and ambiguities of the living-together family need to be addressed. Use clear, concrete language; do not hide behind abstractions. If the relationship is time-limited in that the woman is leaving the state for another job in 6 months, the children should know that. If the couple cannot marry because the man's divorce is not final, the children should know that. These issues need to be honestly dealt with. They should not be a shameful secret or a cause celebre, but a fact of life. Above all, the biological parent needs to attend to the children's needs and feelings. The child who feels he is unimportant or that his needs do not count is learning a very unhealthy lesson. Children are neither all powerful nor powerless. Children are people with feelings, needs, and questions. Be a responsible, attentive, approachable parent.

The partner has an important, but limited, role with children in the living-together situation. He should not pretend to be the permanent parent, take over the disciplinary role, be aggressive or abusive, or make unrealistic promises ("I'll always be there for you"; "We'll go fishing next year"; "I'll coach your team"). He can be a steady, supportive person in the children's lives, a backup for their mother, and follow the same rules as the biological parent.

Dealing With Your Child's Other Family

Children of divorce have two households, their mother's and their father's. One or both parents might be remarried, so the child can be dealing with two stepfamilies. It is a challenge to adapt to the different rules and realities of two households. The parents try to coordinate and follow through on homework, music lessons, sports teams, religion classes. However, things like eating times, a routine before sleep, TV rules, and friends visiting will vary depending on the situation and values of the different households. It is not a "right–wrong" situation but different family styles. Children are capable of understanding and following a different set of routines and rules for each of the two households.

Parents and children should avoid competition and manipulation. The parent needs to maintain appropriate boundaries of who is responsible for what. When the child is at your house, you are the responsible parent. When the child is at the ex-spouse's house, he or she is the responsible parent. Unless there is an abusive or dangerous situation, you have no right to interfere. If you want to coordinate activities or make suggestions, communicate directly with the ex-spouse, not through the child. You are the adults; do not put the child in the middle. This includes not questioning the child about the ex-spouse's life, relationships, or stepfamily. If the child wants to discuss or share things, listen attentively but be non-judgmental about her other family.

It is common to dislike the ex-spouse's new partner. This is not your concern. Stay out of each other's personal, emotional, and sexual lives. Focus only on parenting issues. You did not have influence over the ex-spouse when you were married, so why do you think you can influence him after the divorce? Focus on what you can influence—the child's well-being when she is with you. Do not be judgmental about her care when she is with the ex-spouse.

This guideline is particularly important for the non-custodial parent. Most of the child's time is spent in the ex-spouse's care. When you are with the child, be more than the "fun" parent who entertains the child at movies or on outings. You want to know the child and she to know you, your family, and her extended family. This is the time to share your values, skills, interests, and feelings. It is not the time to negate or undermine her home and custodial family. Use your parental time constructively.

Stepsiblings and Extended Family

There are more relationships in stepfamilies and more variability in these relationships. There are age differences, as well as differences in religious beliefs, academic and athletic skills, and life experiences. The child has new aunts and uncles, cousins, grandparents. Sometimes, close relationships develop; many times these are distant relationships. There is often sibling rivalry, and sometimes angry, even abusive, relationships.

It is unrealistic to hope for problem-free relationships with stepsiblings and extended family. Physical and sexual abuse is more common in stepfamilies than in nuclear families. Do not treat this situation with benign neglect. You cannot force friendly or loving feelings, but you can insist that destructive or abusive relationships be confronted and stopped. At a minimum, people need to be respectful. Even if they cannot be friendly, they must be non-destructive.

The hope is that the child develops at least one supportive relationship—with a grandparent, aunt, stepsibling—so there is a positive connection to the new family. Having additional sources of guidance, support, and nurturing is an advantage of stepfamilies. This includes an older stepsibling who serves as a role model. Children can grow from the stepfamily experience. An example is a 13-year-old girl who was an academic underachiever, math phobic, and did not participate in sports. Her 20-year-old stepsister played soccer, was a math minor, and liked having a younger sister. She agreed to be her tutor and kick a soccer ball around and talk. A strong motivator was visiting for a college weekend and being introduced as my "favorite little sister."

The New Baby

Chapter 8 discusses the issue of whether to have a baby in this marriage. There is something appealing about the concept of her children, his children, and "our" child. The decision of whether to have a baby is an adult decision, based on personal needs, values, and a consideration of whether it would enhance or subvert your marriage.

Ideally, a baby increases family cohesion. This is especially true if stepsiblings are encouraged to take a nurturing role with the new child and do not feel burdened by being a "substitute parent." It is good for older siblings to realize how much attention a baby needs, but it is unfair to burden them with responsibility for the baby. The focus of an adolescent is their academic, social, and personal development. They need freedom to be children rather than be burdened by the responsibilities and worries of adulthood.

A young child needs stimulation, attention, affection, and nurturing. Receiving this from the stepfamily can be of value to both the child and family. A young child helps put conflicts and stresses in perspective. A stepfamily that experienced stress with the father's 19-year-old daughter and 16-year-old son and the mother's 9- and 7-year-old sons found that having a baby was an emotionally-centering experience. Taking care of the baby was gratifying and served to put parenting struggles in a less negative light. Seeing them take care of the baby reminded the other children that they were loving parents. Babies can be enjoyed by both adults and children.

Exercise—Creating a Functional Stepfamily

Most exercises call for assessment and for writing change plans. This exercise involves discussion and family meetings. This is a talking and doing exercise.

Family meetings are particularly valuable for stepfamilies. Everyone attends and hears the feelings, perceptions, opinions, and suggestions of other family members. Adults fear this could become a "tease and taunt the parents" session, but that seldom happens. Families need a predictable way to function. Neither chaos nor an authoritarian structure promotes a healthy family. The goal is to create a flexible, cohesive stepfamily.

The structure of the family meeting is to spend the first half discussing concerns, feelings, perceptions, and problems. The emphasis is on free-flowing communication and active listening. The second part involves reaching agreements and trying new approaches to improve family functioning.

Begin the first meeting by having each person talk about their experiences and feelings when the stepfamily was formed (whether 3 months or 10 years ago). Encourage expression of both positive and negative feelings. What were the hopes and fears about the stepfamily? Talk about what you most enjoy and what has been disappointing or difficult. What do you want from the stepfamily? Examples include a stepfather requesting that the children spend time getting to know their new grandparents, a mother asking the children to help prepare dinner and promising she will teach them to cook, a daughter who wants tutoring her stepsibling to be part of her allowance, a son asking his mother and siblings to attend his soccer games. Requests can range from having at least one family outing a month to asking that a steps-ibling not taunt his younger brother.

It takes most stepfamilies at least a year to develop a comfortable, functional way of relating. Some researchers believe 3 to 5 years is more likely. This process takes time, effort, communication, consistency, and goodwill. The realistic goal is a functional stepfamily, not the idealistic goal of a perfectly cohesive unit.

Once-a-week-family meetings can be valuable. However, it is crucial to avoid turning these into "bitching" sessions. Examples of "bitching" include charges and countercharges among siblings, parents blaming children and children blaming parents, saying none of the problems would exist if the parents had not divorced, and taunting or making fun of family members. The focus should be on expressing feelings, shar-ing perceptions, and resolving issues. Creatively dealing with concerns enhances family functioning. Some issues are resolvable. Some require coping techniques so that the problem does not become worse.

Creative resolution includes rearranging kitchen furniture so that everyone has his or her own space; going on a picnic after 3 hours of family chores; allowing each child to take turns choosing what the fam-ily will do on a Sunday afternoon; rearranging car pools so less time is spent waiting. Problem-solving examples include a schedule for study-ing in the family room; determining when the TV is on and off; deciding which parent monitors which child's homework; the stepparent assum-ing responsibility for Boy Scouts; an allowance system that is reviewed yearly. The best advice for handling difficult issues is to stop obsessing and engaging in "what-if" thinking. Coping strategies include reaching a compromise that makes the situation tolerable, realizing that this is a difficult phase and the situation will change in 2 years; not personalizing problems; entering individual, couple, or family therapy.

Stepfamilies cannot ensure that past successes will carry the fam-ily forward. Developmental, relational, and practical changes impact families. We suggest maintaining family meetings on at least a once-a-month basis. Any member can call a meeting if there is an issue of concern.

Family Cut-Offs

Unfortunately, in some families a person can decide that an issue cannot be resolved or that there is too much pain and disap-pointment, so he "divorces" the family. This includes a father abandoning the children and moving to another state, an adolescent running away from home, a mother moving and sending the child to live with relatives. Family cut-offs occur with teenagers or adults when they identify their families as destructive and think of themselves as adult children of a dysfunctional family.

Negative or traumatic experiences from childhood should not be denied or be a "shameful secret." Groups and self-help books that break the silence and provide validation for dealing with childhood trauma can be helpful. There are self-help groups for Adult Children of Alcoholics, Adult Children of Abuse, Incest Survivors, and Adult Children of Divorce. However, it is self-negating to define oneself as a victim. To say the most important thing about your childhood was "I'm an adult child of an alcoholic" or "I'm an adult child of divorce" is re-victimizing. Life is meant to be lived in the present with planning for the future, not controlled by trauma or anger from the past. You can be an adult survivor, not a victim.

There are situations in which the healthiest approach is to divorce oneself from a father who is destructive, a sexually abusive stepfather, a physically violent stepbrother, a mentally ill mother, an antisocial family environment. This is the exception, not the rule. People who consider cutting themselves off from a parent or the entire family should not do this without consulting a professional—psychologist, family therapist, pastoral counselor. Cutting off a relationship says that it is hopeless, that there is nothing salvageable. Although you may feel angry or desire revenge, you must realize that most relationships and people do not fall into the "evil" category. You are likely to learn more about yourself, relationships, setting appropriate boundaries, and negotiating realistic expectations if you stay with the process, rather than cutting it off by a family divorce.

These guidelines are particularly relevant with adolescents, when impulsiveness, anger, and black-and-white thinking can be dominant. Teenagers are prone to "burn bridges," which they later regret. The tumult and drama that accompany angry cut-offs interfere with the person's development and puts terrible stress on the family. This is especially true when the teenager asks that the parent choose "between me and the marriage." Another unhealthy example is the adolescent who will no longer visit his father, with the mother acting as a cheerleader for the cut-off. Individual and/or family therapy is particularly important in this situation.

RYAN AND NICOLE

Ryan married Nicole when he was 32, Nicole 34, and her sons 8 and 4. Within a year Nicole was pregnant with a daughter, and 2 years later a son. They have been married 7 years, and the children are 15, 11, 6, and 4. Ryan was an optimist who felt they would be a golden family. Ryan read that marrying before the children were 9 was a positive prognostic sign for a stepfamily. Ryan wanted to adopt the stepsons, but Nicole correctly assessed that the ex-spouse would not tolerate it.

During their 7 years of marriage, Ryan tried to do everything right. He nurtured the intimacy, respected and cherished Nicole, was an involved father for his stepsons, coached their athletic teams, and loved parenting the younger children. However, Ryan was stressed and burned out. The core of the problem was that the oldest son was in a rebellious phase, saying he admired the biological father (which incensed Ryan, who felt he had been ten times more caring than the neglectful father). He was smoking and drinking, which Ryan feared was a negative model for the younger siblings. Nicole was less surprised by these changes. Nicole had been a rebellious teenager herself and understood this in her son. Nicole realized life was not as "rosy" as Ryan liked to paint it, and felt prepared to deal with the difficult issues they were facing as the children entered adolescence. Her consistent refrain was "we'll survive this."

Nicole realized that if they let their marriage and family be controlled by the oldest son it would make a difficult situation disastrous. She cared about all four children. She was not willing to ignore the developmental needs of the three youngest children to focus all attention on the problematic son. Nicole and Ryan consulted his guidance counselor and teachers, who assured them this was not a crisis but did require breaking the pattern of low motivation and boredom. They reached an agreement that if he did well in school he could spend the summer with Ryan's sister, who owned a ranch in Montana. This helped break the cycle.

Nicole suggested they take a couple weekend without the children. They hiked, talked, and made love. Nicole was afraid of Ryan "burning out." She reminded him that they had 14 years of parenting left. Ryan felt good about their marriage but drained by career, financial, and especially parental concerns. Was the time and energy they devoted to parenting worth it if this was the result? Nicole enjoyed parenting, especially younger children. She did not expect parenting teenagers to be fun, but realized adolescents need consistent monitoring, guidance, and emotional support. Ryan giving up on his stepson and becoming an alienated parent would only make things worse. Ryan had to find a point on the parenting continuum where he was not overwhelmed with either fear or anger. Ryan vowed to remain the caring parent that his stepson had unfortunately learned to take for granted.

As they walked along the river, Ryan and Nicole discussed how to better balance parenting each child, work, house, family, personal time, and nurturing their relationship. Family life is a dynamic process; you need to be aware of each person's needs and feelings. Things change, so you cannot take the stability of your family for granted. This is the marriage and family Ryan and Nicole wanted and valued, although it was considerably more complicated and stressful than they had imagined. Ryan realized that even though the marriage was intimate and solid, parenting four very different children was challenging. For the family to function well, Ryan and Nicole needed to be a respectful, supportive parental team.

Closing Thoughts

We could write an entire book (and someday might) on the challenges and pitfalls of stepfamilies. The biggest traps are pretending that stepfamilies are the same as nuclear families on one extreme and on the other extreme feeling overwhelmed and devitalized by the inherent complexities and difficulties. Families experience challenges and problems. Yet, the majority of stepfamilies thrive, and the children grow up to be healthy, resilient adults.

The most important bond in a stepfamily is the husband–wife bond. You need to develop a cooperative manner of parenting that takes into account differences between biological children and stepchildren, developmental needs of children, and phases of the stepfamily. There are vast differences in stepfamilies—for example, the couple who married when the children were under 5 as opposed to marrying when the children were teenagers.

Stepfamilies can be functional and satisfying. They require thought, work, communication, and respect for complexity and individual differences. Each family has its unique strengths and vulnerabilities. The stepfamily needs to be accepted for itself, not as a second-class substitute for the nuclear family. Be open to dealing with the realities of your second marriage and stepfamily.

CHAPTER 8

Should We Have a Child?

There are few life decisions that carry greater emotional and practical import than whether or not to have a child. A planned, wanted child is one of life's most joyful experiences. A baby can bring a stepfamily and second marriage together. However, an unwanted pregnancy or a poorly thought-out decision can tear the marriage asunder. The time a couple is most likely to split up in first marriages is 3 months before or after the birth of a first child.

Having a child involves a permanent commitment. You can change jobs, marriage partner, and where you live much easier than giving up responsibility for parenting. Becoming a parent is one of the most complex and important decisions facing a remarried couple. Only you can decide what is best for your marriage, situation, and stepfamily.

We strongly advocate planned, wanted children. Ideally, this decision is carefully thought out and mutual. Too many couples give in to cultural or family pressure to "do the right thing" and have a baby. It is only the right thing if it is right for you. If remarried couples carefully weighed their feelings, preferences and situation, at least half would decide against having a child. The value-ladened assumption that if the partners are loving and secure they will have a baby is wrong. For many couples, the most loving (as well as practical) decision is to not have a child in this marriage.

Myths About Having Children

There are a number of myths about children:

1. The more the merrier.
2. An only child will be maladjusted.
3. You must have your first child by 30.
4. You should not have children after 40.
5. You need a child to bond the marriage.
6. It is crucial to have both girls and boys.
7. Planning children takes love and spontaneity from sex.
8. Children stabilize a shaky marriage.
9. Having a baby cements a stepfamily.

In contrast, we suggest the following guidelines:

1. Having a baby is a choice agreed to by both spouses.
2. The marriage is on solid footing emotionally and financially before the decision is made to become pregnant.
3. The couple is married at least 2 years before having a baby.
4. The child is planned and wanted.

Children are at least an 18-year commitment. Parents have the psychological readiness and financial resources to make that commitment.

Having a baby would not negate commitments to children already in the stepfamily.

The decision to have a baby is emotional and far-reaching. This decision cannot be based on myths or the traditional perception that a baby validates the marriage. Conception is a potential function of sexuality, not its prime function. Children are not necessary to justify sexuality or the marriage. Ideally, a child would be planned and wanted, an affirmation of the couple bond and commitment to the stepfamily. This involves an immensely important, individualistic choice. Barry has counseled competent, successful couples who have no trouble making million-dollar professional decisions but wilt under the stress of a family planning decision. Choosing to have a child is fundamentally an emotional commitment. If couples decided only on the basis of financial and logistical factors, people would not have children.

The primary reasons to have children are to experience the process of pregnancy, be involved in parenting, and watch the child grow into an independent person. Pregnancy, childbirth, and parenting are among life's unique and special experiences. The time—as well as the financial and emotional commitment—children require is truly daunting. Both spouses need to carefully and honestly consider their willingness and ability to make that commitment. How will a child affect the marriage and stepfamily?

Couples who decide not to have a baby deserve to have their choice respected and supported. The decision not to have a child is a positive commitment to individual, marital, and stepfamily growth. Many second marriages and stepfamilies function better without the stress of a new baby. It is a myth that a new baby is necessary to cement the stepfamily.

Making a Decision Based on Current Realities

When college students are asked if they plan to marry, 90 percent say yes, and more than 85 percent expect to have children. At 21 you assume you can do whatever you want and believe everything will work as planned. Few expect to divorce or be faced with the question of whether to have children in the second marriage.

People make decisions based on dreams and hopes of the past rather than on present realities. For example, a 44-year-old woman married a 41-year-old man who had a vasectomy after having two children in his first marriage. She had planned to marry and have children in her twenties. She did marry at 29, but realized it was a fatally flawed marriage. She had the courage to act on this and get a divorce. She was glad she had not had a child with him but was disappointed that she did not remarry until 44. Her thoughts about having a child were the same as at 29, but her life circumstances were dramatically different. Having a first child at 44 raises a number of health issues. In addition, she had an established career; her husband had a vasectomy; she needed to adjust to the new marriage and become involved with stepchildren; he had a different life agenda than starting a new family. Having a baby did not make sense practically or maritally, but it meant she had to give up a lifelong dream.

The decision to have a baby should be based on current and future realities, not on past hopes or dreams. Decisions should not be influenced by "if-only" thinking. Timing is not everything, but it is important. The person who enthusiastically desired a child 5 years ago might not now. The spouse who planned to adopt finds that the agency will no longer accept him because he is over 50. Are they willing to adopt a foreign child? A sad but true adage is that life is not fair. You do not have the luxury of your ideal choice. Make wise decisions based on current realities.

When One Spouse Wants a Child, But the Other Does Not

A common and difficult conflict is that one spouse wants a child but the other does not. There are many things you can compromise on, but a child is something you either have or do not have; there are no halfway measures. Ideally, the couple would discuss this before marriage, but reality is seldom the ideal.

Many couples do not decide and leave it to chance or haphazard contraception. Sometimes one partner makes a unilateral decision (often not revealed to the spouse). The man has a vasectomy or the woman gets a tubal ligation, the woman stops taking birth control pills or discards her diaphragm, the man puts holes in his condoms or stops using them. We do not recommend this.

We suggest you discuss having a child (by yourselves or with guidance from a minister, marriage therapist, or trusted friends) sharing feelings, desires, perceptions, fears, and reality concerns. Rather than a debate or lobbying effort, we urge an open discussion. How important is having a child? What are your motivations and how healthy are they? How feasible is it? What are the fears? Are they realistic or irrational? Is the spouse who strongly wants children willing to be the primary caretaker? Is that doable? Can the spouse accept not having children? Will the partner's life be miserable if they have a child? To promote clarity, we suggest that each spouse put down a number (from 1 to 10) to specify how strong their feelings and desires are. Is the spouse so adamantly opposed that it is a 10, which effectively vetoes the idea? Is the other spouse's desire for a child so strong that he cannot remain in the marriage unless they have a child? Typically, both people are ambivalent.

A major source of ambivalence is whether a baby will reinforce or weaken the marital bond. Ideally, the decision to have a baby is an affirmation of the strength and durability of this marriage. How did having a child affect the first marriage? Many people feel the most positive thing about their first marriage were the children, although they admit that having a baby stressed the relationship.

Another source of ambivalence is when one spouse has biological children and the other does not. The spouse says she will be a better stepparent if she has a child of her own. She feels a need for children. He does not want to be in the position of blocking her needs even if he does not want more children. Decisions about children are not a "tit-for-tat" game in which one spouse keeps score and demands her turn. Disclose feelings, perceptions, desires, and worries. Share ambivalence and reach a decision that at a minimum both can live with and ideally would enhance your marriage and family. The decision to have a child is made jointly, not by the spouse who has not had children.

GINA AND THOMAS

This was Gina's first marriage and Thomas' third. He married at 19 when his first wife became pregnant. They struggled to maintain that marriage through 5 years and a second child. Thomas kept contact with the children even though his ex-wife moved to a different state. Four years later he married a woman with a 9-year-old son whom she wanted Thomas to adopt. Thomas did begin the adoption process, but the boy's father objected. Three years later Thomas was divorced and glad that he had not adopted the boy.

Thomas' children were 11 and 9. Their mother had an alcohol abuse problem that was becoming severe. She had two driving-while-intoxicated arrests that resulted in the loss of her license and job. The children wanted to live with their father.

This was Thomas' first experience as a full-time custodial parent. The longest he had had them previously was 2 weeks. Thomas was honest in saying that a prime reason to pursue the relationship was so Gina would share parenting. Thomas was a better parent at 33 than he had been at 19, but he did not relish being a single parent.

Gina had an unplanned pregnancy at 16 and for religious reasons chose to have the baby, which she placed with an adoption agency. Gina took satisfaction in helping an infertile couple have a child but powerfully felt her loss. Each year on the birthday, Gina would attend religious services and pray for the child's healthy development. At 28, Gina wanted to marry and have a family of her own. She loved Thomas and wanted to be an active stepparent. Her fear, which proved true, was that the ex-wife would want the children back. The struggle over custody arrangements would continue for the foreseeable future. This provided an additional impetus for Gina's desire to have a baby.

Thomas insisted they be married for 2 years before discussing a baby. This would make Gina 30, and she wanted a baby in her twenties. She agreed with his logic that they needed to be sure their marital bond was healthy and stable. Gina enjoyed the parenting role. It was hard to accept that the children did not call her "Mom," but Gina forged a genuine, caring bond, especially with the younger child. In talking to the ex-spouse, Thomas made the point that each child was an individual with her own needs. The older child returned to the mother's custodial care, and the younger child stayed with Thomas and Gina. When the mother's life and drinking regressed, the older daughter returned to her father's home.

Thomas was ambivalent about a baby. He found parenting two children a mixed blessing. Did he want to return to the diaper stage? Was he confident that they would be able to keep their marital and parental commitments? Could they have a "normal" parenting experience with a new child? Gina did not want to manipulate Thomas, but she expressed her feelings and desires. Gina was committed to keeping their marriage viable and secure. This was true whether or not they had a baby. Gina was convinced that having a baby would strengthen their marital bond and facilitate being an emotionally cohesive family. Gina talked of her feelings, needs, and hopes in a way that involved Thomas, but was not pressuring or blaming. Her optimism won Thomas over.

Intercourse with the hope of becoming pregnant energized their sexual relationship. Thomas joked it was a shame it only took 3 months to get pregnant. It is very frustrating to want to be pregnant, have difficulty, and fear infertility. Luckily, getting pregnant was easy, and Gina had a healthy pregnancy. The first people they told were the children. They talked as a family throughout the pregnancy, and acceptance and enthusiasm built.

Gina and Thomas attended a prepared childbirth class. Thomas had not been involved in the birth of his daughters so being present at the birth of his son was very exciting. The birth was a highlight of Thomas' life. Gina was an enthusiastic mother, and willingly shared caretaking. The baby added to the family's emotional cohesiveness. Being parents strengthened their marital bond. This planned, wanted child enhanced their marriage and family.

Two years later, Thomas and Gina discussed whether to have a second baby. This involved examining emotional and practical factors, with each sharing feelings, perceptions, desires, and fears. This time Gina was ambivalent. She loved the baby, but was reluctant to press their luck. Gina felt a strong pull to open a new chapter of her life. This would be a good time to return to school and finish her degree. Thomas was building a business that would generate income for the children's college. If he were 5 years younger, Thomas would have liked another child—the symmetry of two sets of two children was appealing—but the timing was wrong. Since Thomas was more committed to not having additional children, he volunteered for a vasectomy. Gina was sad, but glad they acted on the decision. She had no desire to deal with an unplanned pregnancy.

When the Couple Cannot Decide

Having a baby is a major life choice that deserves time and attention. Guidelines for discussion and decision-making sound straightforward and reasonable, but they are emotionally challenging and difficult. How can you be sure you are making the right decision? Complexity and fear result in paralysis. The stress of ambivalence and indecision makes the marriage miserable. That is why couples play "conception Russian roulette"—they let chance decide.

We suggest several techniques to break the impasse. One is the writing and talking exercise that follows this section. Another is to utilize the services of an uninvolved, but trusted and respected, consultant. It could be a professional such as a marriage therapist, pastoral counselor, psychologist, or a nonprofessional such as a best friend or couple friends, a neighbor or cousin, or a lay counselor from your church. Speaking in front of someone and hearing each other's feedback can focus and crystallize issues. Another technique is to set a specific structure and time frame: for example, talking once a week for ten weeks to explore financial, practical, and emotional issues. If no resolution is reached, you agree to revisit the issue in 4 months using a different format.

These techniques are used to move the process forward, not force a decision. Having a child is too serious a decision for coercion or ultimatums. What about couples who could procrastinate forever? Those couples should seek professional resources, usually marital therapy, to facilitate the decision-making process.

Exercise—Discussion and Decision-Making

This exercise is divided into four components:

1. Each partner individually writes about issues.
2. They share the written material and have a discussion.
3. As a couple, they write about these clarified issues.
4. They engage in mutual discussion and decision-making.

The structure for the writing exercise is that each spouse lists feelings under four columns: 1) positive feelings about having a baby; 2) negative feelings about having a baby; 3) positive feelings about a baby's effect on marriage and stepfamily; 4) negative feelings about a baby's effect on marriage and stepfamily. On a second piece of paper, the partners should focus on practical, financial, and situational factors: 1) positives of having a baby; 2) negatives of having a baby; 3) positive effects on marriage and stepfamily; 4) negative effects on marriage and stepfamily.

Honestly explore both feelings and practical factors. Write this for yourself, not to win over your spouse. Be as specific and realistic as possible. For example, positive feelings might include holding an infant, the sensations of rocking a baby, breast-feeding, the joy of cuddling with a toddler, looking forward to teaching the child to play soccer, the process of watching the child develop, pride in showing the child to her grand-parents. Negative feelings about the effects on marriage and stepfam-ily might include feeling overwhelmed and harassed by a baby, losing couple time and connection, dealing with jealousy and sibling rivalry, feeling tired and depressed, burdened by family responsibilities that will be extended 18 years. Examples of positive practical factors include older children learning to be responsible for a younger sibling, the baby serving as an impetus to move to a larger house, receiving emotional and practical support from the extended family. Examples of negative practical factors include financial stress, less personal and couple time, need for backup and emergency child care, not getting a promotion at work because you cannot travel.

Give your spouse these lists before the discussion. The purpose of the discussion is to share thoughts and feelings, and to be sure each spouse is understood. Do not weigh alternatives, try to persuade the spouse, or rush to a decision. Clarify feelings, perceptions, and concerns. The format is to ask open-ended questions about what was written and to empathically reflect feelings, hopes, concerns, and problems. Clarify positive and negative factors so that you both share the same informa-tion base. Some couples find this mechanistic and tedious, but many are surprised at what they hear and discover. The spouse's feelings and views are more complex and ambivalent than expected. Sometimes the spouse is shocked that she has misperceived his fears and concerns.

The third phase is to jointly write positive/negative feelings and positive/negative practical factors. Writing makes your thoughts con-crete and forces you to approach decision-making as a joint project. Do not worry about the lists being balanced. By this point, there is greater clarity and hopefully a decision. Seldom is it an easy "yes–no." There is usually ambivalence and uncertainty on the part of one or both spouses, although they are able to come to a decision. If not, proceed to phase four.

The couple discussion/decision-making process is difficult. If the decision had been easy, discussions would not have gotten this far. We advise against coercion, ultimatums, or forcing a decision. A baby affects both people, your marital bond, and stepfamily. Express feel-ings and wants. This is the time to advocate, but do so fairly—without threats or hidden agendas.

We advise couples to discuss this issue at least once a week and preferably twice a week for at least 5 weeks and up to 15 weeks. This is not to wear the spouse down, but to seriously examine individual and couple desires and fears with the goal of reaching a mutually acceptable decision. Utilize the subjective 1-to-10 scale to state how strong your desires and concerns are. For example, the ability of one spouse to tolerate not having a child might be a 5. The spouse's fear that a child would disrupt the stepfamily is a 9. Although her desire for a child is 7, she concludes it would be best to have a tubal ligation.

This decision asks you to weigh emotional and practical factors, to decide based on current feelings and your best prediction of what will happen in the future. There is complexity and ambivalence because of the import of and shared responsibility for the decision. No wonder people often leave it to chance or one spouse makes a unilateral decision (to stop using birth control or be sterilized).

What if these discussions do not reach a resolution? You can postpone the decision for a month or a year. Or you can seek outside consultation with a psychologist, marriage therapist, minister, physician, or trusted friend.

The Danger of Not Deciding

The major issues that stress a marriage are money, children, and sex. The emotions that most stress a marriage are anger, alienation, and resentment. These emotions are problematic in the decision-making process but are even more likely if a decision is not reached. The spouse who wanted a child becomes angry, alienated, and resentful because the partner avoided and procrastinated. This is especially true if she believes this was his "hidden agenda." The opposite is true if the pregnancy occurs "by accident." The spouse who was unsure feels manipulated and distrustful. Was it really an accident? No matter how complex and stressful, reaching a joint decision is better than not deciding. If the final decision is not to have a baby, the couple runs the risk of an unplanned pregnancy. This is why sterilization is the most common contraceptive choice for couples in their 30s.

The socially desirable response is to have a child. Parents encourage adult children to have children because that is what they did. People believe children strengthen a marriage and family. Sometimes it is selfish advice—they want to be grandparents (being a grandparent is much easier than being a parent). There is overt and covert cultural pressure to "do the right thing" and have a baby. The more the couple discusses having a child, the more likely they will choose to get pregnant. The spouse who wants a child (usually the woman) is able to overcome the concerns and fears of the ambivalent spouse.

The decision should not be based on social desirability, approval of parents, or pressure from friends. Too much is at stake. The choice should be based on what is best for each spouse, your marriage, and stepfamily. Ideally, you would make a decision that meets all those needs, but it is unlikely; otherwise it would have been easy. Usually, one spouse feels more strongly, and the couple goes with the wishes of the person with stronger desire. It is crucial this be acceptable to the other spouse. Refrain from intimidation, coercion or ultimatums. The marital bond is strengthened by a mutual decision.

Make the best decision given your information, feelings, and resources at the time. If the decision does not work, do not turn on each other. For example, if the baby has a birth defect or is chronically impaired, the reluctant spouse should not blame this on the spouse who wanted a baby. If the decision was not to have a baby and 5 years after the vasectomy the man wishes he had, it is important that the couple not engage in a blame–guilt cycle.

Most decisions are changeable, although at a very high cost. Some are not. Does it help you or the marriage to punish yourself or each other for a poor decision? One of the reasons couples do not make a decision is that they are afraid of making the wrong decision and being blamed. Think out and discuss decisions. Take responsibility for making the best decision you can. This process is healthier if each person is committed to support the decision, avoiding second-guessing the spouse or decision.

Infertility Problems

Infertility problems are unfair in any situation, but especially in a second marriage when you have decided you want an "our" child. For 75 percent of couples, getting pregnant is too easy; for 25 percent it is problematic. Approximately 10 percent of couples (more after age 30) are unable to conceive.

Fertility problems put great stress on a couple, more than an extramarital affair or sexual dysfunction. Fertility workups themselves are stressful. Taking daily basal temperature, keeping track of the high probability period, and being subjected to multiple diagnostic procedures is difficult. Males find it embarrassing and anxiety-provoking to produce a sperm sample on demand, especially in the sterile atmosphere of the bathroom in a physician's office.

It is the norm to experience diminished sexual enjoyment after months of fertility assessments. A significant number of couples develop sexual dysfunction, especially inhibited sexual desire. Fertility problems take the fun out of sex. During the high-probability week, sex is "task-oriented." Many couples stop being sexual, although therapists urge sex for pleasure and reconnection during the rest of the month. Couples need coping strategies to deal with the monthly cycle of hoping that this time they conceived and the disappointment and anger of a menstrual period.

The couple in fertility treatment faces increasingly invasive and expensive interventions. Some couples reconsider whether conceiving a child is worth this. Other couples consider the option of adoption in this country or overseas. These are individualistic decisions depending on people's feelings, values, practical circumstances, financial resources, and psychological factors. We suggest self-help groups and professional resources to help you deal with these issues.

Closing Thoughts

This chapter has provided an overview of the complex issues involved in deciding whether to have a child. That is one of the most important and long-lasting decisions you make. We have suggested guidelines to help in the discussion and decision-making, but it is a very individualistic and subjective personal decision.

We are strong advocates of planned, wanted children and the importance of a mutual decision. Having an "our" child can strengthen the marital bond and stepfamily. However, if not well-thought out or if one spouse is not committed, having a child can tear the marital bond and stepfamily asunder. Be sure psychologically, emotionally, and financially that having a child is in your best interest and will promote the marriage and stepfamily.

CHAPTER 9

Traps and Vulnerabilities

No one ends a marriage without emotional scars. Being aware of sensitivities and vulnerabilities is a crucial step in rebuilding self-esteem and having a successful second marriage. Do not fall into the trap of feeling like a victim. Use awareness to avoid traps and to enhance psychological well-being. You are a survivor; do not act out the victim role.

You learn from the first marriage and divorce. Psychological well-being is enhanced by accepting reality, coping with loss, and learning from mistakes. The unhealthiest response is to feel guilty, lower self-esteem, and repeat self-defeating patterns. Identify positive experiences, accept negative experiences, and be aware of traps and vulnerabilities. For example, a man whose first marriage ended because of his propensity for physical violence takes personal responsibility for the problem. He changes attitudes, behavior, and emotional reactions regarding anger and anger expression. This includes not choosing a woman who is dependent or prone to blame herself. He is honest with a prospective partner, open about his vulnerability, and clear that spouse abuse is not acceptable.

Another example is the woman who left her first marriage after trying for 3 years to convince her husband to seek therapy. He suffered from obsessive-compulsive disorder, and was unable to change. He tried medication, but could not tolerate the side effects. Checking and hand-washing rituals became more severe. She felt guilty divorcing when his mental health was deteriorating, but she no longer respected or loved him. She had an affair, partly as motivation to leave and partly to give a specific excuse for the divorce. She regretted the destructive way the affair played out; it should have ended 10 months before it did. In thinking about remarriage, she had no interest in men with mental health problems. When she discovered a man was taking medication for depression, she terminated the relationship. She did not want to be judgmental, but this was not a problem she was willing to deal with.

Being aware of sensitivities and vulnerabilities is not a sign of weakness or craziness. Everyone has sensitivities and vulnerabilities whether from their family of origin, life experiences, or the first marriage. Rather than denying or minimizing, awareness empowers you to make healthy choices. Part of psychological well-being is acknowledging personal strengths and emphasizing these. In other words, "play to your strengths."

Equally important is awareness of sensitivities and vulnerabilities so they do not subvert your life. For example, a man who has a vasectomy should avoid developing a relationship with a woman who wants children. A woman who is committed to her career and has a history of struggles with men over autonomy should avoid a relationship with a man who espouses traditional values. For some, sharing financial resources is a major value; others want to maintain financial autonomy. One approach is not right and the other wrong, but awareness of vulnerabilities and traps allows you to identify a relationship that is not viable.

The issue of "traps" is especially important in second marriages. For example, the man's first marriage broke up because of financial secrets and misuse of credit cards. In this marriage, he is hypervigilant about his wife's credit cards, suspicious of any financial problems, and overreacts with fear and anger. He is falling into a "trap" from the first marriage, which causes major stress and distrust in this marriage.

Another example is a woman's dependency, which kept her in a fatally flawed marriage for 10 years. In this marriage she is so afraid of becoming dependent that she does not allow herself to be emotionally connected. Her fears control this marriage. Some people fall into the same traps in the second marriage. A male hates "serious talks" because he expects his spouse to complain and blame him. He is too tired to talk and uses sleep as an escape. The current wife loses respect for him and both withdraw emotionally. It is a disappointing and alienated marriage heading toward divorce.

It is important to be aware of self-defeating traps but even more important to have a coping strategy that ensures you will not repeat these traps. For example, as his first marriage ended, a man finds that masturbation is an easier, more predictable way to meet his sexual needs than couple sex. He discloses this trap to his new wife and commits to a regular rhythm of couple sex, only masturbating when he is out of town. The woman whose trap is avoiding financial discussions because the ex-spouse would berate her for being stupid about money attends a course in financial management with her new spouse. They meet each month to discuss the family budget and make financial decisions. Dealing with traps is a one-two combination: being aware of and monitoring the trap (with your spouse's help), and devising a specific strategy to change the pattern.

Traps and Vulnerabilities Are Normal

Everyone has his or her "demons"—vulnerabilities, sensitivities and traps. People with the highest psychological well-being and most satisfying marriages have traps and vulnerabilities. The issue is not whether you have them, but how you deal with traps and ensure that they do not control your life and marriage. On a personal note, our marriage was simpler in that we had a similar trap from our families of origin. Both fathers used violence and threats of violence as a means to control the spouse. We made a premarital agreement that we have honored throughout our relationship: not to engage in intimidation or violence. Each person is responsible for changing attitudes and behavior. The spouse can help by supporting the change process.

How important for the success of the second marriage is coming to grips with one's "demons"? It is vital. Disclose problems and develop a monitoring system so you remain accountable. For a variety of reasons, sometimes the spouse is unwilling or unable to serve in that role. Enlist a friend, minister, therapist, sibling, sponsor from a self-help group—someone you trust—to help you monitor and change the pattern. You need not feel guilty or shameful about personal demons, traps, and vulnerabilities. However, you are responsible to ensure that they do not control your life and marriage.

Many people feel victimized and traumatized by their first marriage, especially by how it ended. Do not view yourself as a victim and act out the victim role. You are a survivor who deserves to thrive. This does not mean denying trauma, stuffing feelings, or pretending it was easy. It means carefully reviewing negative experiences, thoughts, and emotions at the time and in retrospect. Acknowledge that you survived, did as well as you could, learned from the divorce and are committed to being a survivor. "Living well is the best revenge."

EDIE AND JOHN

Edie was 32 years old, in her second marriage, and the custodial parent of a 14-year-old daughter and a 7-year-old son. John was 39; this was his first marriage, although he had lived with a woman for 5 years. Edie and John had been married 1 year and entered therapy to decide whether to have a child.

Edie was clear about her vulnerabilities and traps. She had been in individual therapy to deal with the decision to leave her first marriage, reorganize her self-esteem, and be a single parent. Edie's unplanned pregnancy was the reason for entering a fatally flawed marriage. Her decision to have a second child was a badly thought-out attempt to save the failing marriage. Edie asked her first husband to leave while she was pregnant, and he responded by taking an overseas job and not sending child support. Although a dutiful parent, Edie did not find parenting satisfying and questioned whether she wanted to try again with a third child. Could she handle an adolescent and a baby?

John had developed a positive, nurturing relationship with the stepson but realized he had little hope with the stepdaughter. John did facilitate a relationship between his mother and stepfather and the daughter, which Edie appreciated since she was estranged from her parents. John wanted family stability to give his life a sense of meaning. This was his mother's third marriage and John had stopped counting for the father. John had been sent to boarding schools and therapists since he was 9 years old. He wanted stability, had no faith in therapy, valued this marriage and desperately wanted it to work. This desperateness was one of his traps. Edie questioned whether he valued her or was he driven by insecurity.

The therapist kept John and Edie focused on understanding and changing personal vulnerabilities rather than trying to change the spouse. The first agreement was to continue using contraception for 6 months to give them the time and freedom to carefully assess individual, couple, and stepfamily factors in deciding whether to have a child. This meant Edie could explore personal plans, feelings about the marriage, attitudes toward parenting, and the possibility of a baby without feeling pressured. John had an opportunity to examine the healthy and unhealthy sources of his motivations. Personal exploration within the context of respectful, non-judgmental couple sessions was very helpful. When John stopped making demands of Edie, he found she did value him and had confidence in them as a couple. This was especially important since parenting the daughter was more stressful than John had imagined. Edie and John agreed to go out as a couple once a week and have a weekend without the children at least every 6 months.

They discussed career and financial issues. Edie dreamed of starting her own business but had not been in a position to realize this dream. John was a government employee who enjoyed his job and received merit bonuses. A baby would mean Edie would have to postpone her career dream. She could not imagine juggling a baby and a new business. John considered whether he wanted a baby for the right reasons or to provide a socially acceptable role. John was surprised to learn that couples without children reported greater marital satisfaction.

John's parenting time and energy was with the stepson, not as a rejection of the stepdaughter but with realization of the limited role he played in her life. The stepfamily functioned better when these roles were realigned. Edie was the primary parent, which was what the daughter wanted. John developed a calmer, cooperative relationship with his stepdaughter. John's involvement with the stepson gave him the parental role he wanted. A baby felt less necessary.

John and Edie talked as trusted confidantes and explored each other's vulnerabilities in an accepting rather than competitive manner. It is hard to self-disclose unless you trust that your spouse has your best interest in mind. As John and Edie shared feelings, perceptions, fears, dreams, and plans they felt closer and more trusting. Although they had disagreements, these were no longer threats to the marital bond. After 4 months of therapy, they agreed that since Edie was the spouse most certain that she did not want another child she would have a tubal ligation.

The decision not to have a child was mutual, made with ambivalence and regret (seldom are life choices made without hesitancy or uncertainty). This freed John and Edie to have satisfying personal, professional, and couple lives, as well as be better parents to the two children.

Not Falling Into Traps

It is easy to repeat past mistakes and act out self-defeating patterns. Vowing not to do so or making "New Year's Resolutions" is not enough. Be aware of problematic cues and high-risk situations. Even more important is a specific plan to engage in healthy, functional behavior. For example, the man who reacts to loneliness by turning on the TV and being passively entertained is repeating a pattern that started in childhood and has played out through two divorces. If he is not going to let this subvert his current marriage, he needs a specific plan to deal with loneliness and boredom. Since it is a longstanding, dominant pattern, change will not be simple. It is easy to resume old habits, especially when stressed or discouraged. He will need a specific plan, someone to monitor and reinforce the changes (usually the spouse), and be accountable so the inevitable lapses do not turn into relapses.

Changing behavior requires motivation and discipline, including setting non-perfectionistic goals. When he feels lonely or bored, he engages in healthy alternative activities (prepares a dinner by himself or with her, reads a novel or magazine, goes for a walk by himself or with a neighbor, tells his wife he is bored and suggests a joint activity). At the beginning of the week, he circles the TV programs he is interested in and only has the TV on for those programs. When the program is over, he turns the set off rather than "channel surf" or watch whatever is on. He asks his spouse to monitor his TV watching and reinforce non-TV activities. When feeling lonely or stressed, he pushes himself to do something healthy; passively watching TV feeds isolation and depression.

Non-perfectionistic goals are particularly important. Some traps require total abstinence. Abstinence is easier than moderating a behavior. It is easier to stop smoking than to smoke five cigarettes a day.

Most traps are moderated, not abstained from. People cannot abstain from feeling angry, embarrassed, overeating, feeling disappointed, or withdrawing sexually. These are patterns to monitor and moderate, not behaviors that demand abstinence. Plans for change reduce problem frequency and intensity but do not require perfect behavior. Perfectionism is bound to fail. Individuals and couples can and do make significant changes in self-defeating behavior patterns.

Exercise—Personal Vulnerabilities and Couple Traps

This is a writing exercise to be done alone and then shared with your spouse. Be honest. Disclosing vulnerabilities strengthens the trust bond. You trust that the spouse respects you with your weaknesses and vulnerabilities, not just for your strengths and stellar characteristics. What you disclose will be honored and not used against you.

In assessing personal vulnerabilities, review sensitizing events and problems from the family of origin, life experiences, and the first marriage. Remember, everyone has traps. An unhealthy response is to deny problems and pretend you are perfect. Self-esteem is anchored by acknowledgment of personal strengths, positive experiences, relationships, and competencies. You promote well-being by your ability to accept negative personal attributes, vulnerabilities, unsuccessful or guilt-inducing experiences, being hurt or rejected, and areas of incompetence or inadequacy. You can admit vulnerabilities without sacrificing self-esteem. These are not "crazy" or "fatal flaws," but a normal part of being human.

Examples of vulnerabilities include being a poor money manager and building debt; causing the marriage to end because you were immature and irresponsible; jealousy and fear because of a prior spouse's extramarital affair; not completing college, which limits career opportunities; having a history of phobic or depressive behavior; growing up in a dysfunctional family; being embarrassed that police were called to your house in the first marriage; chronic sexual dysfunction; a problem with gambling or insomnia; tendency to become depressed and avoidant.

Place each vulnerability into one of two categories: problems you can change and those you need to accept. Vulnerabilities such as poor money management can be addressed by taking a financial management course (by yourself or with your spouse) or designing a money management system that eliminates all but one credit card with a modest credit line. Some problems, such as a chronic sexual dysfunction, are better addressed by seeking therapy. Individual, couple, sex, group, or family psychotherapy is not a sign of weakness. Working with a therapist can be the most efficient and effective means of resolving a problem and reducing vulnerability.

Some problems are not amenable to change or require too much time and investment to be worthwhile. The best strategy is acceptance. Not every problem or vulnerability has a solution. In accepting vulnerabilities, be sure they do not dominate self-esteem or subvert this marriage.

The second part of the exercise asks you to honestly and carefully assess traps that could subvert this marriage. Be aware of a prevailing pattern of self-defeating behavior, especially when feeling depressed, anxious, or stressed. What repetitive, self-defeating traps do you fall into?

Keep a separate list for individual and couple traps. Self-defeating patterns are played out in both realms. Awareness of traps is a crucial first step, but if you stop there you lower self-esteem and make it more likely you will fall into the trap. Prevention is the best way to deal with traps. Identify high-risk cues and situations. If the trap for the male is to lash out angrily when feeling disrespected, he should identify high-risk situations. He specifies effective ways to deal with these, including awareness that it was not the spouse's intention to put him down. He takes responsibility for angry thoughts and realizes these make the situation worse.

In developing healthy alternatives, he needs to learn three strategies: 1) anger management skills—changing thoughts and utilizing relaxation techniques so anger does not accelerate; 2) learning to identify and disengage from the anger cycle by calling "time out" or going for a walk; 3) confronting physically abusive or out-of-control anger and realizing that no matter what the circumstances it is harmful and unacceptable.

The woman's trap is feeling overwhelmed, depressed, and guilty because she cannot make everyone happy. She withdraws and feels taken advantage of. Her hard work and caring is taken for granted. She cries by herself or complains to female friends but does not deal directly with the spouse. She has seen this pattern with her grandmother, mother, and in her first marriage, and is modeling this for her daughter. The best intervention is prevention; she needs to set healthy limits so she can balance individual, career, marriage, parenting, and household time. When experiencing role overload, she changes the pattern. She builds self-esteem on a solid base of adult competencies and accomplishments, friendships, and family relationships. She acknowledges strengths and her worth. She requests an equitable sharing of household and parenting tasks.

She needs to look at what she does for the children. Are there things they could do independently, or could she teach them to be more responsible? Assigning specific chores for children is helpful in their development. Feeling taken for granted is aimed at the husband, not the children. He is an adult who should know better. When feeling depressed and undervalued, she can vent those feelings verbally or in writing to her spouse. She needs to engage her husband, couple friends, individual friends, relatives, or a therapist in a problem-solving approach to the role overload. She is open to positive reinforcement for herself and receiving it from others.

Every couple has traps. The traditional trap is the woman pursuing the man, wanting more contact and communication. He withdraws, resents her criticism, and fights to maintain his autonomy. This is the "pursuer-distancer dance." Another trap is the man making elaborate family plans and the woman feeling put upon because she has to organize everyone to implement them.

List three couple traps. Do not try to script your spouse's behavior. What can you do to change your role in perpetuating these traps? These are your commitments, regardless of what your spouse does. Do not make a "tit-for-tat" agreement saying you will not do something as long as the spouse refrains from his problem behavior. These lead to perpetuating the pattern with attack–counterattack about whose fault it is that nothing changes.

Once you have completed the list, share it in a respectful, caring manner. Give supportive, specific feedback and suggestions that facilitate the change process. Focus on changing two couple traps. Each partner makes a personal commitment to break the cycle and an agreement to pursue a healthy alternative.

Living As a Survivor, Not a Victim

In the 1950s American culture glorified the family and family unity. During the 1990s, there has been a rise in the Victimization and Adult Child movements, and the claim that 97 percent of American families are dysfunctional. The pendulum has swung from one extreme to the other. These trendy shifts ignore the complex realities of people's lives. Traumatic, sad, rejecting, confusing, and emotionally painful events occur in the family of origin and during marriage and divorce. No one has a picture-perfect, idyllic childhood or a "perfect" life. No one goes through a divorce without emotional scars.

"Silent victims" deny and dissociate from painful emotions and experiences. Awareness of vulnerabilities and traps is a crucial step in the healing process. Being an "angry victim" who defines her self-esteem by the abuse does not promote healing. It is not healthy for you (or your children) to be stuck in the victim role. Learn to think, feel, and behave as a survivor who deserves to succeed. A victim feels controlled by the past, reacts in a self-defeating manner (whether passive or angry), feels ashamed and burdened, has low self-esteem, and is prone to repeat self-defeating patterns. A survivor objectively assesses past experiences, accepts the sadness and pain, learns from problems without feeling guilty or putting herself down, is committed to living in the present and building self-esteem, monitors and changes traps, and takes pride in being a survivor. Life is meant to be lived in the present, not controlled by the pain and disappointments of the past. You are not a hopeless, helpless victim of divorce. You are a proud survivor who has learned a great deal about herself and coping and is committed to living well.

It is your responsibility to be a survivor, not your spouse's role to make you one. Good intentions and saying the right words are not enough. Be aware of vulnerabilities and traps (especially from the first marriage), commit to not repeating these patterns in your life and second marriage. You deserve a functional life and are willing to put in the time and effort to achieve it. You can develop a specific change plan, realistic goals, and a system to implement and maintain healthy changes. Your spouse is an integral part of the change process. She can help maintain motivation, be a monitor, positive reinforcer, and share pride in the changes.

Dealing With Lapses and Regressions

The change process only works perfectly in movies and self-help books. Everyone experiences lapses; do not allow this to become a relapse. The most self-defeating reaction is to give up in disgust, losing self-respect and the respect of your spouse. Another self-defeating pattern is to regress and deny there is a problem. The essence of the marital bond is respect. This is subverted by denial or pretending.

Not all problems are changeable, but most are. For example, one spouse has been a smoker for 20 years and has unsuccessfully attended five smoking cessation programs. He agrees not to smoke inside the home. The hope is he can muster motivation for a program that is better designed, and that he can be successful. Maintaining a healthy weight is one of the most difficult traps (both Barry and Emily struggle with this). Giving up and regressing to unhealthy, out-of-control eating is self-negating. Even if the problem does not get substantially better, you need to ensure that it will not get worse. Being "stuck" is frustrating, but regressing is worse. You owe it to yourself and the marriage not to give up.

Couples hope to share their lives forever. This means they will go through stressful times in which problems seem insurmountable. This can last for days, weeks, months, or even years. When Barry listens to couples remarried for more than 20 years discussing their lives, he is struck by how different the problems seem in retrospect. He remembers a couple joking about the 7 years they parented stepchildren. It was difficult but worthwhile. The relationship with their adult children is fairly good, and they do not blame each other for past problems. Parenting adolescents is difficult, especially in a newly formed stepfamily. Everyone survived, and they enjoy the grandchildren. Those were difficult times, but they persevered. Take pride in not giving up.

Trust in the Second Marriage

Respect and intimacy are important, but trust is the crucial ingredient when discussing vulnerabilities and traps. When you self-disclose, will the spouse respect your vulnerabilities and be supportive? Will the marital bond remain intimate and stable? Answering affirmatively is crucial to trust.

How much can and should you disclose about problems, vulnerabilities, and traps? Ideally, you would disclose all sensitive issues and do so before marriage. Focus on them; you need not disclose all the embarrassing details. Establish guidelines and be open to feedback on how the spouse processes and responds to self-disclosure, especially emotionally painful topics. Some spouses are uncomfortable and do not want to engage in these discussions. Others are opinionated and tell you what you "should" feel or do. Some use this information to explain relationship problems as your fault, causing you to feel betrayed and put down. Others complain theirs is no longer an intimate relationship, but one dominated by problems and over-analysis. If these are the reactions, full self-disclosure is inappropriate; it will not facilitate well-being in the marriage.

How do you want your spouse to respond? You want him to be a respectful, non-judgmental, caring listener. You want vulnerabilities honored and to feel close and trusting. You share yourself—wants, fears, traps, and all. What is your intention? Do you want him to listen, offer alternatives, problem-solve, be your advocate? There is a big difference between solicited and unsolicited advice. Is the solicited advice helpful? If you are not open to unsolicited advice, will she heed that? Is there mutuality in self-disclosure, or is it one-way? Couples find sharing feelings and experiences valuable. Do not compete or one-up each other. Share feelings, sensitivities, and vulnerabilities. Enjoy the enhanced emotional intimacy and trust.

Do you trust that this marriage will remain stable and satisfying? People remarry with the hope that the marriage will endure, but not with the certainty they felt in the first marriage. The greater the marital trust, the more comfort with self-disclosure. In Barry's clinical practice, one of the saddest moments involved a couple who had disclosed painful, emotional vulnerabilities. They tried to save the marriage, but realized it would end in divorce. How will the ex-spouse treat the sensitive information? Divorcing couples must not abuse each other's disclosures. However, especially in contentious divorces, painful disclosures are thrown up to the spouse during depositions or court hearings. That is unfair and sad, but there are no guarantees in life. In a viable marriage, disclosing feelings, experiences, and vulnerabilities builds and strengthens the marital bond.

Closing Thoughts

Each spouse brings traps and vulnerabilities to the new marriage. Being aware of and sharing makes it less likely that traps will subvert your life and marriage. Do not see yourself as a victim or act out the victim role. You are a survivor who deserves a satisfying life and second marriage.

CHAPTER 10

Understandings and Agreements

The two most important strategies for creating and maintaining a healthy marriage are setting aside couple time and developing understandings and agreements. In this chapter, we will guide you through communicating openly to arrive at shared understandings, both as a couple and as a family. Reaching agreements is a critical skill, especially for second marriages. People come to second marriages with a history of successes and disappointments. It is all too easy to force past solutions onto the new marriage. Some might fit, but most will not. Your spouse is a unique person. Be aware of how he or she approaches life, marriage, communication, and values.

Assumptions about the marriage can cause major problems if they are not checked out and revised. For example, one woman assumed her new husband would appreciate gourmet cooking, but he enjoyed simple meals on the grill. Another example is the husband who assumed that since he made more money he should have veto power over expenditures. The wife was determined to be a serious, equal financial partner and would not accept unilateral vetoes.

The key is sharing information, perceptions, and feelings in an open, non-defensive manner. Avoid arguments based on the myth that there is one right way to do something, and if the spouse does not agree he or she is wrong. In law, science, and business there are clear data-based rights and wrongs. When it comes to marriage, feelings, perceptions, and preferences are crucial. There are a variety of ways to deal with children, organize a kitchen, interact with friends. "I'm right, you're wrong" arguments tear at the marital fabric. They raise heat but shed little light on understanding your spouse, facilitating communication, or problem-solving.

Understanding your spouse's feelings and attitudes is just as important, and often more important, than the content of the discussion. Empathy is crucial. Empathy means understanding the viewpoint and feelings of the other person. Empathy allows you to put yourself in another's shoes and see the issue from his vantage point. Understanding and caring sets a solid base for dealing with problems. This is especially important when there is major disagreement over a difficult issue. Knowing you understand and can validate your spouse's feelings makes it easier to discuss alternatives and problem-solve.

The Four-Step Agreement Process

The understanding and agreement process involves four steps:

1. Share feelings, information, and perceptions in an empathic manner.
2. Explore a range of alternatives.
3. Problem-solve and come to an agreement that has a good chance of resolving the issue.
4. Implement, monitor, and alter the agreement so it is successful.

Couples want to rush the process so that the problem is resolved and out of the way. Quick, painless solutions are often not an option; many problems are emotionally charged, complex, and not amenable to a simple solution. These problems need to be addressed in a serious manner. Carefully proceed through each step. Expressing feelings, hopes, and fears while being listened to in a respectful, empathic manner is healing. It sets the stage to deal with issues as intimate team members who trust and respect each other.

The second step is to develop and discuss alternatives. The key is being open to creative solutions that address and can resolve the problem. Some problems have only two or three reasonable alternatives. Frequently there are practical and emotional factors that allow multiple perspectives. It is important to generate alternatives in a creative manner. Most involve a "mosaic" solution, taking parts from each spouse's suggestions.

The third step is to reach an agreement that is acceptable to both spouses and has a reasonable chance of succeeding. At a minimum, each spouse can live with the agreement. It is not intended to undercut or hurt one spouse. Rather, it is hoped that the agreement will resolve the problem and serve the needs of both spouses. The "win–win" outcome is ideal, but it is important to be realistic. Not all agreements meet each person's needs.

Stay away from the "tit-for-tat" format. An example is the wife who agrees to take the husband's children to the family reunion if the husband agrees to visit the wife's parents monthly. Neither wants to do this and feels coerced. The typical outcome of "tit-for-tat" agreements is a draining power struggle that results in neither person getting what he or she wants, generating blame and resentment.

The Positive Influence Model

We advocate a "positive influence" model of reaching understandings and agreements. Express feelings and needs, but do not push them on your spouse. An agreement that is in the couple's best interest is more important than getting your way. Do not force your solution at the expense of spouse or marriage. To do so wins the argument but loses the relationship. The positive influence process recognizes the value of a respectful, trusting couple bond.

Traditionally, males have lobbied for the rational, cost-effective resolution and did not attend to the emotional aspects and costs. Females have traditionally tried to please their spouses and reach a resolution that meets everyone's needs (except theirs). She does not attend to practical dimensions and ensure that the resolution is viable.

In the positive influence model, couples do not assume rigid, traditional roles. Practical and emotional factors are important to both people. The well-being of the marriage and advancing the process are more important than either "feel-good" or "cost-efficient" agreements. We emphasize trying to make "wise" decisions—taking into account both emotional and practical factors to come to a resolution that is helpful in both the short and long term.

You cannot have it all, no matter how many alternatives you look at or how much negotiating you do. You can reach a good agreement that addresses the concerns of both spouses, moves their lives forward, and improves the situation. In some cases, the agreement stops the situation from degenerating further. In many instances, an agreement adds joy and confidence to the marriage and converts a problem into a source of strength and pride.

The fourth, and most overlooked, step is to implement, monitor, and modify agreements. For an agreement to work there must be an action plan and follow-through. Good intentions and New Year's resolutions can cause damage. Change is seldom easy or straightforward. The positive influence process includes monitoring and modifying agreements. Successful implementation increases trust and respect for the spouse and marriage.

The trap couples fall into is that they become discouraged and give up when an agreement is not followed or there is a regression. She blames him and questions his motivation. Even more self-defeating is to feel, "If you really loved me you would do this perfectly." Remember, human behavior is complex. There are reasons something is not working. Perfectionist goals are an enemy of change. With sports-minded clients, Barry uses the analogy that "in his best year Ted Williams only hit .407." Couples are encouraged to stay with the agreement and monitor and refine it until it works well (not perfectly). A suggested monitoring format is keeping written records and having short bi-weekly or monthly meetings to assess problems, make changes, and set goals.

Exercise—Designing Positive Agreements

Few couples have formal written agreements. However, they are surprised to discover they have implicit or informal agreements about a number of matters. Examples of informal agreements that enhance the marriage include: during visits to extended family going off for 2 hours to enjoy a couple hike; sitting down once a month to review family finances; attending stepchildren's athletic activities at least once a week; having breakfast in bed and reading the Saturday paper; going for a run together after a stressful day; having a family picnic after Sunday religious services; going away for a weekend without children at least once a year; every other Saturday night playing bridge with couple friends; doing chores in tandem for 2 hours on Wednesday night.

This exercise involves establishing two new couple agreements. What understandings and agreements would strengthen your intimate bond? Each spouse is free to state needs and make requests. Agreements could involve major issues such as moving to a larger house or sending a child to a different school. The agreement could be a mundane life change such as a different system for doing grocery shopping or determining how the children's baths are handled. You could develop an understanding involving something of symbolic significance such as reaffirming loving feelings through touch and/or words at least three times a week. An emotionally meaningful understanding is talking to family and friends in a manner that shows you value the marriage. Consider practical agreements—who brings in the morning paper, drives the inconvenient car pool, takes the time to make a healthy snack.

Each spouse creates a list of three to five requests. Each person chooses one to develop an understanding/agreement, so you have two agreements to design and implement. Each agreement stands on its own. Stay away from "tit-for-tat" agreements that become bogged down in conflict over one spouse not doing her part, so the other spouse stops doing his. "Tit-for-tat" results in paralysis and resentment. Positive agreements move the process forward and increase marital satisfaction.

Carefully go through the process: Listen empathically to your spouse's feelings and perceptions, develop a list of alternatives, have a clear agreement that both spouses can accept, and a monitoring system to ensure that the agreement is successfully implemented. All four steps are crucial; if one is ignored the agreement will probably fail.

The most ignored step involves implementation and monitoring. Good intentions are not enough. A system—formal or informal, oral or written—needs to be in place. The system we recommend (and use in our marriage) is to place the agreement where it is readily accessible (on the desk, refrigerator, or nightstand). Once a week set a date to talk about the agreement and how it is working. You could do this sitting on the porch, on a walk, or over a cup of coffee on Sunday morning. Design a monitoring system that works for you. Otherwise, the agreement will lapse or fail, no matter how positively you feel about it. Hope for change will turn into frustration and disappointment. If the understanding and agreement were important enough to make, you owe it to yourself and the marriage to reap the benefits of successful implementation.

Agreements, whether about mundane or major issues, are an energizer. Knowing you can positively influence your spouse raises confidence in your relationship. Realizing you have the motivation and ability to go through the process of listening to each other's feelings and perceptions, discussing alternatives, reaching a mutually satisfying agreement, and successfully applying it increases respect and trust. Reaching understandings and agreements is a resource you probably did not have or did not utilize in your first marriage.

The Importance of Problem-Solving Agreements

Agreements are healthy for a marriage. Yet, even in the best of marriages, there are problems and tough issues. Problem-solving agreements are just as important as positive agreements, and even more necessary.

Agreements help even if they are not ideal. You will not get all you want. "Compromise" is a word we hear a great deal, but it is not one of our favorite concepts. What happens with compromises is that neither partner gets what he or she wants, and the issue is not successfully addressed. The classic example is that one person wants to go to a Chinese restaurant, the other wants Italian food, and they "compromise" on a mediocre fast food restaurant that neither enjoys. It takes time and energy to go through the process of stating feelings, needs, and perceptions, creatively exploring alternatives, developing an agreement, and successfully implementing it. However, it is a worthwhile investment. Agreements are vastly superior to compromises. Your marriage will move forward (and you will eat better too).

Everyday hassles and problems tear at the marital fabric. People believe that major problems or crises destroy a marriage (loss of a job, a child dropping out of school or running away, an extramarital affair, alienation from in-laws, illness). These are major stresses, but researchers have found that the everyday problems and disagreements most stress the marriage. Preventing conflicts and problems is optimal, and sometimes understandings and agreements can be used proactively. However, many problems cannot be prevented, and they have to be dealt with. Conflict management skills are among the most important in marriage. Problem-solving understandings and agreements are a vital marital resource.

Exercise Two—Problem-Solving Agreements

Start by reviewing previous agreements—formal and informal—to deal with differences, conflicts and difficult issues. This heightens awareness of what has and has not worked. A word of advice: do not use this exercise to refight old battles or demand retribution for bad agreements.

Be aware of individual and couple patterns in approaching conflict. There are several traps couples fall into: both spouses avoid dealing with a problem until it is a crisis; one spouse is a relentless negotiator, while the other gives in; one spouse is always identifying complaints and the other minimizes problems; the couple talks an issue to death without reaching a resolution; they promise to do better, but are not committed to a change plan; they settle for "feel-good" agreements that duck the difficult issues; one spouse writes down all the agreements, but neither spouse looks at them; she gets her way, but his passive–aggressive stance subverts the agreement. Do you fall into these or similar traps? Be sure your problem-solving process addresses these issues.

This exercise requires each spouse to identify three everyday problems or hassles that interfere with the marriage. The spouse chooses one to develop a problem-solving agreement. They design two agreements, one from each spouse's list.

The four-part process used for positive agreements is even more important for problem-solving agreements. Begin by stating feelings and perceptions. Avoid the "guilt–blame" trap; focus on agreements for the present and future. Listen in a respectful, caring manner, especially to your spouse's fears and worries. Be aware of the problem and its impact. Attend to both content and feelings.

Be clear about your intentions and motivation. Both spouses need to trust that there are no hidden agendas, no manipulation, and no intimidation. The problem-solving agreement should be based on honesty and the positive influence process. The goal is to resolve the problem. The agreement is not at the expense of your spouse or relationship.

Neither partner is trying to put something over on the other, or get her way at his expense. When that happens, you win the argument, but lose the goal of maintaining a respectful, trusting marriage.

In discussing alternatives, be open to each other's ideas, suggestions, and modifications. Ensure that the agreement meets both practical and emotional needs. There is not one right way to solve problems; find what works for you.

Be sure the agreement addresses the concerns of each spouse. You want an agreement that has a good chance of working and, just as important, that allows the partners to see themselves as a team committed to successful implementation. Most problems do not have perfect resolutions, and for some there is no good solution. However, there are always positive alternatives (a mosaic solution).

For the first two problem-solving agreements, pick issues that can be improved easily rather than the most intransigent problems. Do not try to deal with the ex-husband's late financial payments or court threats. Your spouse has little control or ability to change that. Choose issues such as an agreement about monitoring children's homework; sharing chores so that the lawn gets mowed and the garbage taken out; avoiding interminable battles over whose fault it is when something is wrong; creating a workable money management system that makes it easier to do the monthly budget; determining which extended family events both of you need to attend; balancing couple and individual time; dealing with car or house problems so work is minimally disrupted.

Being able to make and implement problem-solving agreements is a major source of marital strength. It gives both people confidence that they can address daily hassles as well as major problems. Dealing with tough issues and seeking improvement is a better goal than striving for total resolution. Knowing issues will be addressed before they reach crisis proportions is reassuring. Problem-solving agreements serve as a valuable marital resource, increasing trust and respect.

Issues That Cannot be Successfully Resolved

There are always alternatives but not always successful resolutions. For example, a 14-year-old might have no interest in forming a bond with his new stepfather. However, you have to parent him. Inability to reach a good resolution does not mean you give up.

Mother is the prime parent, and the biological father hopefully continues contact (that is something you cannot control). The stepfather does not become the "heavy" or the enforcer/disciplinarian. Hopefully, he establishes a connection with his stepson. A good alternative would be a "favorite uncle" role as a positive model, confidant, supporter, and helper in navigating the challenges of adolescence. Often that is not feasible. The stepfather and stepson develop a relationship somewhere between the unhealthy extremes of the uninvolved, critical role and the indulgent "buddy." Mother cannot do it for them.

The problem with "pop psychology" is that there is always an easy answer. Some dilemmas facing second marriages and step-families do not have happy resolutions. Not only is the answer not simple, there is no satisfactory answer. Can you accept reality without feeling demoralized and deficient? We suggest the guideline of the serenity prayer: "Have the courage to change what is changeable, the serenity to accept what can't be changed, and the wisdom to know the difference." For things that cannot be changed it is important to develop coping strategies so the sad reality is not overwhelming. Deal with the problem as best you can. This frees you to focus on understandings and agreements that enhance your personal well-being, marriage, and stepfamily.

MICHAEL & LISA

This was a second marriage for Michael, who was 41 and had joint custody of his sons, ages 9 and 7. It was Lisa's third marriage, and she had sole custody of her 6-year-old daughter. They met at work when Michael was the head of a consultation team and Lisa was the division chief. Each was impressed by the other's competence and professionalism and was aware of a mutual attraction.

Michael loved being married and a father, and was devastated when he discovered the ex-spouse was having an affair with a neighbor. Michael sought individual and couple therapy in increasingly desperate attempts to win her back. However, it takes two people to maintain a marriage. He could not save the marriage alone.

Three years after the divorce, Michael was on reasonably amicable terms with the ex-wife, and they cooperatively co-parented. They maintained clear boundaries, and did not become involved with each other's personal or emotional lives; they discussed only parenting concerns. Lisa requested that Michael's ex-wife only call the house in times of emergency. Michael meets with the ex-wife every month to go over financial, planning, and school matters. He discusses parenting issues on the phone during work hours.

Lisa is 44 and has no contact with the first husband and little contact with the second husband (the daughter's father who lives out of state). He does not make child support payments. Lisa had been agitated and bitter about the ex-husband's irresponsible behavior. After much legal expense and at Michael's urging, Lisa ceased efforts to enforce payments. This was hard to accept, but Lisa felt better when she no longer obsessed about the ex-husband's financial irresponsibility.

Lisa struggled with how much she should trust Michael and the viability of this marriage. In addition to the usual stresses of a two-career family, Lisa felt an unfair burden because Michael was gone at least 1 week a month on consulting contracts. Although Michael was an active, involved father who enjoyed parenting, Lisa was irritated that she was responsible for his sons when he traveled.

Instead of consulting a therapist, which Lisa opposed, Michael suggested they see a pastoral counselor who had a reputation for his practical problem-solving approach. Michael had been raised Presbyterian, but attended the Episcopalian church where he found the church support group for divorced and widowed people of great value. Lisa's previous religious experience with a fundamentalist church had been disastrous. She found the Episcopalian congregation open-minded and non-judgmental. She especially liked the minister, who was divorced and remarried.

Michael and Lisa entered a ten-session problem-solving group conducted by the pastoral counselor. This framework fit well because it was similar to how they conceptualized and dealt with issues at work. Michael and Lisa needed to reach agreements about two ongoing problems— how to share chores when the boys were at their house and how to plan couple time. The two major issues were whether Michael should adopt Lisa's daughter and whether they should combine finances or keep them separate.

The counselor suggested they focus on the practical hassles first. He had them record what actually happened at the house the week they were a three-person family, the week they were a four-person family, and the week they were a five-person family.

Evaluating the data was an eye-opener. Michael and Lisa were not aware how differently the household operated in each scenario, and realized there needed to be continuity. They developed an agreement about chores, which was placed on the refrigerator. The daughter was particularly pleased because she felt burdened by the confusion. She now knew what to expect; her chores stayed the same. Michael agreed to double up on chores the weekend before he went on trips. The boys knew what was expected of them whether or not their father was there.

Michael wanted more couple activities, especially going to movies, an occasional weekend hike in the mountains, and staying overnight at a bed and breakfast. Lisa objected, and Michael felt confused and hurt. In discussing feelings and perceptions, Michael was surprised to learn the basis of Lisa's concern: it made her daughter feel unwanted because couple activities were scheduled only when they were a three-person family. Michael wanted Lisa's daughter to feel more a part of the family by staying with her new grandparents (Michael's parents). His sons were close to their grandparents so Michael assumed the daughter would enjoy the opportunity for closer contact.

The husband–wife bond stabilizes the stepfamily. It is important to put time and energy into nurturing and reinforcing your relationship. Setting aside couple time is crucial, whether to take a half-hour walk on a weekday night or a weekend without the children, to hike, go antiquing, and make love. Michael agreed that they would leave all three children with the grandparents. Luckily, both the grandparents and the children were enthusiastic about this plan.

Reaching understandings, making agreements, and seeing positive results were encouraging. As Michael and Lisa began talking about the two major issues, the counselor and other couples in the group suggested it was really one issue: should they trust that this marriage would be stable? If so, Michael would adopt the daughter and Lisa would feel secure in combining their financial resources. Michael revealed how devastated he felt when his marriage broke up and how hard he had fought for joint custody. He wanted to adopt Lisa's daughter, but needed assurance that the marriage and family would be permanent. Lisa disclosed how vulnerable and financially taken advantage of she had felt. She lost more than $50,000 in her first marriage and double that in the second. She was terrified of a third divorce and the financial ruin that would entail. Revealing fears increased intimacy. Adoption would increase the daughter's sense of acceptance and security. Michael was not the kind of person who would take personal or financial advantage of Lisa. What was needed was not a formal agreement, but expressing feelings and reinforcing the trust bond. The counselor suggested a 6-month followup appointment to be sure the understanding and agreement process continued.

Agreements for Stepfamily Problems

Agreements are not just for the couple. They can be used with in-laws, stepchildren, and relatives or friends from the first marriage. Agreements can and do alleviate difficult situations. For example, a grandmother from the first marriage wants to keep contact with her grandchildren, even though her son seldom sees the children and does not pay his child support. Rather than go through a draining emotional struggle, set up an agreement (preferably in writing) about when the children can visit, for how long, and the practical and financial arrangements. The grandchildren should not be caught in an uncomfortable struggle. Usually it is easier to deal with grandparents than ex-spouses. Children cannot have too many grandparents.

Be sure agreements do no harm. It is easy to be angry and propose an agreement that meets your needs and compensates for past hurts but at the expense of your spouse, children, or ex-in-laws. For a brief time you feel triumphant, but it is a false victory if it harms others. Develop agreements everyone can live with. Agreements get the situation "unstuck" and moving in a positive direction.

The hardest issues involve dealing with children. Scheduling family meetings and writing specific agreements for curfews, grades, work, and buying clothes can be helpful. What do you do with the child who wants no part of it, the teenager who says, "You're not my parent. If you don't let me do this I'm going to live with my father"? Family therapy is a much-used resource for step-families precisely because of these difficult, complex issues. Family therapy helps clarify feelings and expectations and confronts self-defeating patterns. The desired outcome involves understandings and agreements that meet the needs of each family member and promote family functioning.

Even outcomes facilitated by family therapy are imperfect. Sometimes the difficult reality is that there is no good solution. Traditional, rigid control does not work in modern American culture. Positive influence and agreements are healthier than aversive control. Unfortunately, some adolescents and young adults do not act in healthy, responsible ways. After age 18, the parent cannot save the young adult from himself. For most, life experiences and maturity make a difference and the young adult gets his life on track (even if not the track the parent wished). Some never get on track, and there is a sad or even tragic outcome. Adolescent struggles are stressful for the individual, marriage, and stepfamily; however, you do not want this to control your marriage.

Parenting is a major life responsibility with joys and disappointments. Stepparenting is more challenging and difficult than parenting in nuclear families. This makes the process of reaching understandings and agreements even more important. Focus on what will help in the present and future; do not be motivated by guilt, compensation for the divorce, or past parenting problems.

Closing Thoughts

The process of increasing awareness and understandings so that couples and stepfamilies make good agreements is a crucial resource. Respect and trust between partners increases when they share feelings, wants, and perceptions; develop alternatives; problem-solve; reach agreements; and successfully implement them. Devote the time and energy necessary to develop healthy understandings and agreements in your marriage and stepfamily.

CHAPTER 11

Dealing With the Ex-Spouse

The ideal divorce scenario involves no children and an ex-spouse who moves overseas. Unfortunately, reality is that financial, parenting, and emotional battles continue after the divorce. More than 50 percent of ex-spouses remain angry 10 years after the divorce. The ex-spouse is a greater stress on the second marriage than stepchildren. In this chapter, we will look at the type of relationship people commonly have with their ex-spouse and offer some guidelines for thinking about and dealing with an ex-spouse. The goal is to move on with your life and focus your energy on the present.

Although no rule applies to all people and situations, the guideline is not to intervene on behalf of an ex-spouse. Because of your couple history, plus fear about parental rights, the ex-spouse is likely to be defensive or resentful. You should remain detached from the personal, psychological, and relational life of the ex-spouse, wish him or her well, but avoid trying to be the rescuer. It is likely to backfire and make things worse for your relationship, which makes it more difficult to successfully co-parent.

Now, for the really hard issue. What if the spouse's dysfunction interferes with his or her capacity to parent? This turns a sad
situation into a high risk one for your children. Examples include
an alcoholic spouse who drives with children after drinking, a
spouse who is so depressed that she does not cook or take care of
the children, a spouse who spends money on drugs or gambling
so nothing is left for the children's needs, a spouse who engages in
high-risk activities that threaten the children's well-being.

Are you in the best position to assess and evaluate this? Probably
not. Enlist the services of a professional (social worker, minister,
alcoholism counselor), trusted friend, neighbor, ex-spouse's good
friend) or relative (grandparent or sibling) to visit the home and
independently assess the situation. This is especially important (as
well as sensitive and difficult) if there are suspicions or allegations
of physical abuse, sexual abuse, or neglect. Traditionally, the topic
of abuse was shrouded in secrecy, silence, and denial. The pendulum has swung to a point where allegations of abuse are used as a
threat or ploy in child custody battles. Abuse and neglect are very
serious issues that need to be addressed in the best interest of the
child, with no hidden or manipulative agendas.

The Friendly Ex-Spouse

The friendly ex-spouse represents an unusual, but one of the most
difficult, patterns. It is usually the male who wants to be friendly,
especially if he is the one who initiated the separation. He wants
easy, hassle-free access to the children and to feel good about the
past. He offers advice about money, house, kids, cars, and even
his ex-wife's new relationship. His stance is that there is no reason
for hard feelings. Everything has worked out for the best; let's be
friends.

You do not want the ex-spouse as a friend. Why give him influence over your life? He is right that it does you no good to be consumed by anger or a desire for revenge. An emotionally neutral or
cordial relationship has advantages. However, being friendly has
few advantages and a good deal of risk. Why take the chance?

The biggest disadvantage of such friendship is that it gives
the ex-spouse power over your personal and emotional life. A
close relationship with the ex-spouse sets up a potential comparison and jealousy situation if you remarry. If single, it is easy to

become emotionally dependent on him. Will that help your self-esteem? Another disadvantage is blaming yourself for the divorce. Thinking about "what if" or "what could have been" is a drain. This is exacerbated by an ex-spouse who blames you under the guise of friendly feedback.

Not all friendly ex-spouses are men. Barry remembers a woman who offered to feed the dog and watch the house when her ex-spouse went away for the weekend with his new girlfriend. She wanted him to remarry to relieve her guilt at leaving for another man. He hated being patronized. Focus on your own life. Do not react to the emotional needs or agendas of the ex-spouse.

Ideally, you would only deal with an ex-spouse about parenting issues. Stay away from discussions about the marriage, whose fault the divorce was, personal or sexual issues, your current life and relationships. Do not try to establish a friendly or confidante relationship with an ex-spouse. These result in emotional turmoil and refighting old battles, even if they begin with the best intentions. You cannot expect validation or support from the ex-spouse.

The Angry Ex-Spouse

The angry ex-spouse is by far the more common pattern. She blames you for the divorce, resents the divorce settlement, wants to refight old battles, and continues to be angry. These feelings are played out in financial and parental battles. Family court judges throw up their hands in dismay when dealing with couples who are in court every 6 months. Divorce has not allowed them to emotionally disengage.

A key question is: how much of the anger is about the past and how much about current issues. You divorced because you do not respect or trust the ex-spouse. Divorce means he has a very limited role in your life. Usually, the anger is primarily about the past. You cannot control the behavior or emotions of the ex-spouse, but you can control your behavior and emotions. Does feeling or expressing anger from the past serve a healthy need in the present? Does reacting to the ex-spouse's anger serve any positive function? Anger builds on itself. The "catharsis" theory of anger—i.e., get it out and anger will be reduced—has been disproved. The opposite is true. The more you think about, feel, and express anger, the angrier you become. Anger expressed is anger reinforced.

What is the best way to reduce nonproductive anger? The technique we recommend is "cognitive restructuring." It allows you to look at the ABCs of your responses. A is the stimulus, B is your beliefs (thoughts), and C is your consequent behavior and feelings. If B involves angry thoughts about the divorce and ex-spouse, you remain caught in the anger cycle. If you restructure beliefs so that the divorce is in the past and does not control your life, then the consequence is emotional detachment and feeling in emotional control. Psychological energy is focused on current issues.

How should you react to anger initiated by the ex-spouse? The best strategy is detachment. Do not allow yourself to be drawn into angry struggles. As with other guidelines, it is easier said than done, but it is doable. For example, if the ex-spouse begins an angry tirade during a phone conversation, be rational, assertive, and low-key. This is not a healthy or productive conversation. End it by politely hanging up (do not slam the phone down). Avoid conversations with relatives, friends, or people at work about how irrational or unfair the ex-spouse is. Bartenders earn their tips by listening to patrons endlessly play out and justify anger. Fights with the ex-spouse are self-defeating; detach from them.

What about anger involving a current situation? If you carefully analyze it, you will discover that much of this anger comes from the past. You need not deal with an ex-spouse about anything except parenting and following through on financial agreements. Whether anger is directed at the ex-spouse's drinking, laziness, manipulation, poor career choices, relations with relatives, mental health problems, the truth is that you cannot do much about it. If you could not influence him when you were married, how are you going to influence him when you are divorced? It is not your problem.

The hope is that you can establish and maintain a reasonable (not perfect) financial agreement with the ex-spouse. Make the arrangements as clear, specific, and easy to administrate as possible so you are not constantly renegotiating. If the ex-spouse does not live up to his financial commitments, examine viable alternatives. Anger interferes with problem-solving.

Parenting is a complex issue. The biggest trap involves children caught in the middle of their parents' angry feelings. That is unfair to the children and unhealthy for you. The child has two homes, Mom's home and Dad's home. The rules and norms are not the same. You are in charge of parenting when the child is in your custody; do not try to control parenting when the child is with the ex-spouse. That is not ideal, but it is reality. If angry fights continue, our suggestion is to see a family therapist whose subspecialty is parenting in divorced families. The therapy is focused and time-limited. This as an opportunity to resolve specific parenting issues, not reenter into conflicts about the divorce.

The Dysfunctional Ex-Spouse

The dysfunctional ex-spouse represents a difficult and potentially tragic situation. Although some people gloat and say "I told you it wasn't my fault," most are saddened and worried when the ex-spouse is functioning marginally or worse. The problem might be depression, alcoholism, unemployment, suicidal feelings, medical problems, bankruptcy, a second divorce, alienation from family and friends, drug abuse, compulsive behavior. What responsibility do you have to the ex-spouse? Because he is the father of your children, should you try to help?

Exercise—Detaching from the Ex-Spouse

These guidelines sound straightforward, but they are difficult to implement in the complex reality of people's lives, divorce, and remarriage. This exercise is to facilitate a clear, objective evaluation of your relationship with the ex-spouse. The goal is to establish guidelines that promote a realistic, healthy detachment. We suggest you write this and share it with a trusted confidante (parent, spouse, best friend, therapist, minister, sibling). Develop a written set of guidelines that are easily available for use when you are upset or angry.

Review the separation and divorce process. Who initiated the divorce? Was your reaction anger, sadness, regret, happiness? Was there ambivalence and attempts at reconciliation, or was the divorce cut and dried? Were there violent or out-of-control incidents? Was there subsequent sexual contact (one in three couples has sex post-divorce)? When was the worst time in the separation–divorce process? How did you feel and what did you do? Almost everyone has experiences or feelings that cause shame or embarrassment. Have you forgiven yourself?

Draw a timeline and list incidents of over-involvement and reactivity. The trend should be toward expending less energy on negative feelings (anger, depression, blaming, guilt, fear) and less time dealing with the ex-spouse. Especially avoid the attack/counterattack and justify/defend modes.

As you review the notes and timeline, think about what you have you learned about yourself and how to detach from the ex-spouse. What strategies and techniques have been most valuable? What are the traps to monitor so you do not get caught in emotionally draining, self-defeating struggles? The divorce ended your personal relationship with the ex-spouse. The best strategy to reinforce closure is emotional detachment.

The second part of this exercise is more important. What is your current involvement with the ex-spouse? Keep a diary for a month. In one column list all contacts with the ex-spouse—whether a 1-minute phone call or a 2-hour meeting at your child's school. Note the amount of time, type of contact, and topic. In the second column, note your thoughts and feelings in anticipation of the meeting. Did you feel hurt, anger, dread, neutral, sad, anticipation? How intense were those feelings? In the next column, note how focused the contact was. Did you stay on the topic or did you discuss personal issues, the divorce, relationships, political or neighborhood news, share information about extended family? What was your emotional state, and how intense were the feelings? Afterwards did thoughts, feelings, and conflicts about the ex-spouse distract you? If so, for how long and how intensely?

As you review the data, do you find a problem dealing with the ex-spouse? The goal is to have minimal contact, focus on parenting issues, and maintain a sense of detachment. If there are problems, review your records to identify high-risk situations and interactions. Red-line those and develop specific strategies to reduce frequency and intensity. Examples include writing the ex-spouse a note rather than arguing over changing when children are picked up; turning on the answering machine instead of fielding angry phone calls after 10:00 P.M.; making a specific assertive response to get back on track rather than refighting old battles; having your spouse write child support checks rather than becoming angry each month when you write the check; dealing with the ex-spouse by letter or planned discussion (not in front of the children); not discussing the divorce unless there is a therapist or minister present to keep the discussion productive; not interacting with the ex-spouse if she is drinking. The goal is for both people to agree to abide by the guidelines. However, even if the ex-spouse does not agree, follow the guidelines for yourself.

Redo this exercise every 6 months until you achieve an acceptable level of detachment. If the relationship with the ex-spouse remains a problem, consider individual or group therapy.

Relationship Between the Current Spouse and Ex-Spouse

It is very easy to set up a "saint–devil" comparison between your new spouse and the ex-spouse. Like most dichotomous thinking, this does not facilitate honest communication or problem-solving.

Your current spouse can be helpful in putting conflicts with the ex-spouse in perspective, providing emotional support, and offering practical help and suggestions. However, you cannot expect her to rescue you. Responsibility for dealing with an ex-spouse is yours, not your children's, your spouse's, or your parents'. Your spouse can be a consultant and supporter, but cannot take over your responsibilities.

Some ex-spouses want to share observations and secrets with the new spouse under the guise of "telling her what she's getting into." It is your responsibility to share your weaknesses and vulnerabilities. You do not want her blindsided by unsolicited information from the ex-spouse. If painful or embarrassing information is revealed, it does no good to defensively deny everything. Fully share information and discuss perceptions and feelings. Do not exacerbate the situation by engaging in a cover-up or trying to "finesse" the truth. The ex-spouse often takes the role of the worst critic, who attacks your personality and integrity. Counterattacking is not a healthy response. Honesty about the past might be painful, but it is vital. You want to establish a respectful, trusting second marriage. Attacking the ex-spouse diverts you from that goal.

The new spouse and ex-spouse do not become friends, and that is as it should be. There is little advantage, and a number of risks. The new spouse and ex-spouse should interact around stepparenting, not other issues. Of course, there are exceptions to any guideline. People tell stories of two women divorced from the same man who become best friends or a new spouse and ex-spouse who play on the same community basketball team. These are rare situations.

How Partisan Should Your Spouse Be?

Is the role of your spouse to be an impartial observer, supporter, cheerleader, or aggressive advocate? This depends on a number of factors, but the guideline is that your spouse functions as an emotional supporter who helps put the situation in perspective. Being the impartial judge is not appropriate. You and your current spouse should support each other and promote your marriage. Being the aggressive provocateur is harmful; it makes an already difficult situation worse.

Be empathic and supportive in helping your spouse deal with the ex-spouse. Do not be neutral; you are her supporter. Be aware of what she is asking of you—to be a sounding board and to discuss feelings, generate alternatives, provide emotional support, problem solve, and be an intermediary. You might be tempted to offer unsolicited advice. Do not do so, unless your spouse is open to hearing that advice. Maintain personal boundaries. The ex-spouse is not your problem.

Maintaining emotional detachment allows you to provide your spouse with a broader, more objective perspective. Be a helpful consultant. Effectively dealing with the ex-spouse allows you to put time and energy where it belongs, toward your lives and marriage.

JOE AND DONNA

This was a second marriage for both Joe and Donna. Joe, 44, and Donna, 41, had been married for 4 years. Joe had a 14-year-old son, whom he saw each weekend, and Donna had two daughters, 11 and 9, who lived with them. Joe had an amicable relationship with the ex-wife, who had 2 young children by her second marriage. Donna had a difficult, tumultuous relationship with the ex-husband.

Joe was an active, involved father to both his son and stepdaughters. Joe's biggest struggle was not pushing for custody of his son. Donna helped Joe accept that his son's desire to stay in the same school with friends and not leave his mother's house was not a judgment about Joe's worth as a parent. Joe was pleased with the relationship he established with the ex-wife. Donna reminded Joe to maintain appropriate boundaries. Otherwise, he would do things like offer to babysit the ex-wife's two children. Donna felt Joe's role as a "good guy" made it easy for his ex to take advantage of him. She wanted him to devote time and energy to their marriage.

A major struggle was whether to have a child. Joe was enthusiastic, but Donna felt three children were enough. She enjoyed childbirth, but her life was moving along an independent road personally and professionally. Returning to the baby-and-diaper phase had no appeal. After sharing feelings and a good deal of discussion, Donna underwent a tubal ligation. Joe was disappointed but accepted the decision.

Dealing with Donna's ex-spouse about money and parenting was full of stress, conflict, and resentment. Donna had initiated the divorce. There was no easily defined issue like an affair or spouse abuse; rather, it was feeling that she was in the marriage alone. More than 90 percent of the responsibility for the children, household, contact with family and friends had been Donna's. The ex-husband had a bad temper and was critical and distant. Donna realized that her life would be better alone than married to him. The ex-spouse resented the divorce and blamed Donna. He remarried a year before Donna, but that marriage ended within 2 years.

Joe was optimistic that he could resolve problems between Donna and the ex-spouse. Joe's offer to take over dealing with the ex-spouse was fine, although Donna worried about what that would say about her if Joe succeeded. Would the ex-spouse alter Joe's opinion of Donna? She need not have worried. Joe got nowhere. The ex-spouse was a bitter man who lived in the past and had a million excuses why he could not be responsible and consistent with child support and visitation. Joe made a total reversal. He was now Donna's advocate. Donna felt pressure to be more confrontational and punitive than she felt necessary. She did not want to exacerbate these chronic problems or feel pushed by Joe. It was her ex-spouse, not his.

Donna's anger at the irresponsibility of the ex-spouse disrupted her life, especially family finances. She took the advice of a close friend who was an accountant. Donna and Joe's family budget did not include child support payments from the ex-spouse. They established contact with a paralegal at a family practice law firm. Each month in which a payment was not received the paralegal wrote a certified letter to the ex-spouse. If he was 4 months behind on payments, court proceedings were initiated. When money did arrive it was put in a special fund for the daughters' education (or emergencies), minus the payment to the law firm. This was far from an ideal, or even acceptable, resolution, but it was the best they could realistically accomplish.

Joe's role with the daughters was an emotionally loaded topic. Joe did not pretend to be their biological father but wanted them to think of him as the "good" father figure, a role he relished. This put the daughters in a loyalty conflict and enraged the ex-spouse. Donna was helpful in defusing these struggles. The daughters called Joe "Big Dad."

Dealing With Acute Crises

One of the worst things about crises is that one is never prepared. The crisis comes from an unexpected direction and at a particularly bad time (there is really no good time for a crisis). Examples include the ex-spouse losing his job, the ex-mother-in-law dying and the need to make arrangements for the children to attend the funeral, a child's health or school problems causing a disruption in your life, your marriage or the ex-spouse's marriage breaking up. What can you expect of the ex-spouse? How can you ensure personal boundaries are not violated?

Do not expect the ex-spouse to function as a best friend, and do not try to put him or her in that role. It is hoped that the ex-spouse will react in a helpful, problem-solving manner. Focus on the immediate crisis; do not use the crisis to reignite old wounds, fights, or hopes. Deal with the crisis and maintain appropriate personal boundaries. You would feel empathic if the ex-spouse was diagnosed with cancer. However, do not offer to be an emotional or practical source of support; it is not your role.

Trying to rescue an ex-spouse is inappropriate and is unlikely to work. The more likely outcome is an emotionally draining fight about blame and guilt, with you feeling burdened and angry, and the ex-spouse feeling abandoned and bitter. Our guideline is to remain detached and maintain personal boundaries. Wish the ex-spouse well, but do not try to be a best friend or helper. Remember, a special relationship no longer exists.

Chronic Stress Involving the Ex-Spouse

Unfortunately, chronic problems are common. Between one-quarter and one-third of relationships between ex-spouses degenerate into a chronic stress situation. That is sad but true. Even when the ex-spouse leaves the area, there is fear something catastrophic will happen. You have to deal with the children's feelings, their questions about why their father (or mother) does not visit or send birthday cards. If the ex-spouse is in prison, alcoholic, or mentally ill, share that information with the children in a non-stigmatizing, non-frightening way.

A major stress is dealing with an angry, alcoholic, or threatening ex-spouse. The advantage of an acute crisis is that you can focus and it is time-limited. Even though distressing and frightening, it is temporary and hopefully resolvable. There is no such hope with chronic problems. The goal is not a resolution but learning to cope with and contain the stress.

A major trap is "what-if" or "if-only" thinking. Rather than accepting reality, you wish or hope the situation was different. Things would be fine if the ex-spouse stopped drinking. However, you had no control over his drinking when you were married. Why would you have influence when you are divorced? The ex-spouse who is depressed, phobic, under-functioning, impulsive, or a gambler might or might not change. You are better off to assume that the problems will continue. Your task is to reduce the stress caused by this chronic problem. There are things in life, and the ex-spouse is one of them, that no amount of wishing, therapy, prayer, and "if-only" thinking will change. The strategy is not to expend time and psychological energy on the ex-spouse and her problems. Accept the reality, and expend minimal time and psychological energy. Focus on aspects of life in which you have influence and can derive satisfaction.

Potentially Dangerous Situations

This is the most worrisome scenario. If you are afraid that the ex-spouse could hurt you, your children, or members of your family, a psychology book is not the appropriate resource in this situation. We urge you to consult the police, an attorney, and/or a domestic violence program. You need a concrete plan if there is a safety crisis.

These guidelines are meant to reduce the threat of violence. No matter what the circumstances, violence is never an acceptable alternative. People try to justify violence by saying that they were lied to, manipulated, that the spouse had an affair and humiliated them. This does not justify violence. Violence takes a bad situation and makes it ten times worse. No matter what the provocation, the responsibility for the violence lies with the perpetrator.

Most violence occurs at home. Often the only witnesses are the children, which can cause psychological damage. A practical guideline is to have another adult at the home when the ex-spouse is there. This could be a neighbor, an in-law, or a sibling, A better suggestion is to meet or exchange children at a public place—library, YMCA, restaurant—where violence would not be tolerated.

Treat a violent incident with the ex-spouse in the same manner you would a violent incident with a stranger. It is a crime; call the police. Talk of calling the police is usually a hollow threat, which serves to accelerate the conflict. If there is a violent incident, call the police immediately. If there is more than one violent incident, follow through on charges no matter what the ex-spouse promises, says, or threatens.

Closing Thoughts

Dealing with an ex-spouse is one of the hardest aspects of the divorce process. It is important to maintain realistic expectations. Guidelines are that you should emotionally detach, maintain appropriate personal boundaries, and involve interaction only around parenting. Being angry at the ex-spouse or refighting old battles is self-defeating and takes energy from where it is needed—your life, marriage, and parenting.

CHAPTER 12

The Imperfect Marriage—
Surviving Hard Times

It is hard to wake up and realize your second marriage is in trouble. This was not supposed to happen. You confronted fatal flaws of the first marriage, had the courage to divorce, learned from your mistakes, and made a healthy partner choice. How can this marriage be having hard times?

Any marriage will work as long as things are easy. The true test of marital viability is your ability to deal with disappointments, conflicts, and hard times. There are built-in stresses for the second marriage, especially dealing with an ex-spouse and stepfamily. You can expect problems and hard times; be willing to deal with them. If you believe the fantasy that "love is enough" or "if we love each other we'll never have problems," this marriage will not survive the hard times.

All marriages, including ours, are imperfect. All marriages, including ours, have conflicts and difficulties. Some problems can be anticipated and prevented, but not all. This chapter will focus on two particularly challenging areas: dealing with ambivalence about a second marriage and special challenges of parenting in stepfamilies. We will help guide you in deciding which problems you can change and which you can accept and cope with. Most important, we discuss staying committed to resolving problems together.

Many couples enter a second marriage with unrealistically high expectations. This will be the perfect marriage to compensate for the pain and disappointment of the first. They will conquer any and all problems. We stress the importance of positive motivation and expectations, but these need to be tempered with a strong dose of realism. Willingness to address conflicts and hard issues is crucial for a successful second marriage. Stresses and difficulties are best viewed as a challenge, not a negation of your personal worth or the value of this relationship.

The same three major issues that plague first marriages confront subsequent marriages—money, children, and sex. These are often more complicated in second marriages, especially financial and parenting issues. Couples need to talk more and work harder to make this marriage satisfying and stable. A common refrain is "it's not fair—this shouldn't be so hard." Fighting reality subverts emotional stability. Second marriages are harder, but are worth the time and energy investment. You develop self-esteem and pride in the marriage as you navigate and survive hard times.

Money is more complicated because you have to deal with the ex-spouse, especially if children are involved. It is easy to resent the ex-spouse, and blame him or her for your financial problems. It is tempting to engage in "if-only" thinking—if only the ex-spouse paid child support, if only $500 a month did not go to alimony, if only the ex-spouse would sell the house. It makes little sense to stay in an attack–counterattack mode about things you cannot control. Almost 50 percent of ex-spouses remain angry 10 years after the divorce as they refight battles about money, parenting and whose fault it was that the marriage did not work. One reason you got divorced was so you did not have to deal with that person. Do not allow financial struggles from the first marriage to dominate financial issues in this marriage. Accepting reality allows you to reduce the emotional and practical power of the ex-spouse.

Parenting and Stepfamilies

Emotionally and practically, parenting is a major challenge. The worst case scenario is that children become pawns in angry power struggles with the ex-spouse. Equally harmful is that children learn to manipulate parents. When motivated by guilt or an urge to compensate, parents make poor decisions. Guilt is not in your best interest. Although the child takes advantage of the guilt-ridden parent, it is not in the child's long-term interest to have a guilty parent who tries to compensate. Both the parent and child need to accept the reality of the divorce and stepfamily.

What is the best case scenario? Are stepfamilies better than nuclear families? Some unrealistically upbeat writers say of course, but empirical and clinical data demonstrate that indeed there are more pitfalls and problems in stepfamilies. We advocate a realistically positive approach. The best case scenario is that the child maintains a positive relationship with the biological parent and establishes a relationship similar to a favorite aunt or uncle with the stepparent.

Barry recalls a case in which a family therapist was seeing a woman, her ex-spouse, and their three children. The wife and her current husband asked for a consultation with Barry for a second opinion. The new husband felt excluded even though the children lived with them. The ex-husband had remarried a woman who had custody of her two children. The original five-person nuclear family no longer existed as a functional entity. This form of family therapy did not make sense and confused the children. They had two families: a five-person family with the mother and stepfather and a seven-person family with the father, stepmother, and two stepsiblings. Children harbor unrealistic fantasies about bringing the parents together so things could "be like they used to." The family therapist was inadvertently reinforcing this fantasy of the nuclear family.

A common misconception is that the marriage broke up because of the children. Divorce is an adult decision. Children neither cause divorce nor promote their parents' remarriage. You do not say that just once to a child at age six; you need to repeat it with greater sophistication when the child is 9, 12, 15, 18, 21, and in adulthood. Be an "askable parent"; listen to both the content and feelings of the child's questions. Speak to the child at her level, keeping content and feelings congruent. Do not say her father is a sweet man when your anger at him is brimming over. Tell the children that in his role as a father he is concerned and loving, but you are disappointed or angry at him about adult matters.

Parenting is a complex, energy-consuming, full-time job. Babies are so obviously dependent; this is also true of 4-year-olds, 11-year-olds, and 17-year-olds. Caring for children is a very time- and labor-intensive activity.

A shift in parenting occurs at 12 or 13 and continues through young adulthood. The family is less central in the adolescent's life when peer relationships and becoming his own person are core issues. This is a particularly stressful time for stepfamilies, and many parents (especially stepparents) give up in frustration. Arguments between ex-spouses and between biological parent and stepparent about rules and discipline accelerate, partly because the child is being coached by his peers. Teenagers often test the rules and manipulate one parent against the other. He threatens to run away or live with his father. Conflicts over curfews, driving, school, relationships, money, drinking, sex are prominent. Parents wish for the "good old days" when the issues were simpler, like how to keep him active instead of stuck in front of the TV. Teenagers need parenting, even if parenting is no fun.

Our favorite parenting analogy is to equate it with an emotional bank account. You want to establish a positive emotional bond with the child so there are regular, small deposits of emotional goodwill in the parenting bank account. In adolescence, there are fewer deposits, and some big emotional withdrawals. You do not want to run out of emotional capital before the child leaves home.

Adolescence can be a stressful period. Parenting at this phase can also be stressful. When a stepparent enters a family before or during adolescence, the positive emotional bonds have not developed. The stepparent faces the most difficult time in parenting without benefit of a history of a nurturing relationship.

It is crucial to maintain a sense of priorities. The first priority is your personal well-being; no one is helped if you do not take care of yourself. The second priority is your intimate bond, the most important relationship in a family. The parent–child bond is also a priority; it is crucial to be responsible and loving parents. The traditional trap was the child-centered family in which the marriage was ignored and the adults (especially the mother) had their entire self-esteem tied to the successes and failures of the children. The new trap involves self-focused adults who ignore children and parenting responsibilities. Maintaining a healthy balance is essential.

Ambivalence in Marriage

Ambivalence is an important concept that refers to experiencing mixed feelings. There is a desire for the marriage to work, but these vie with negative feelings about the spouse and the relationship. You wonder if it is worth it. Marriages are particularly tenuous when both spouses are ambivalent.

One person cannot carry the marriage. Both need to value an intimate partnership and be motivated to address and resolve problems. One of the hardest issues in marriage therapy is to keep the couple motivated to deal with difficult problems until some understanding and resolution is reached.

Ambivalence is normal, especially when the marriage is stressed and experiencing hard times. It is not what you dreamed of. It is difficult to accept the reality of a spouse who is not as professionally successful as you hoped, not as good a cook, less demonstrative, overly concerned about children from a first marriage, obsessed with work, spends too much money, is not sexually responsive, devotes too much time to his mother, is anxious or depressed. A continuous state of ambivalence is not good for you or your marriage. Stability and security are a bedrock of marriage. It is hard to feel secure when the spouse is constantly weighing whether to stay or leave. Ambivalence detracts from and drains marital satisfaction. To resolve the ambivalence, both partners must decide whether to commit to the imperfect marriage and enjoy its benefits. Resentment about weaknesses cannot be allowed to control feelings toward your spouse and marriage.

The "pursuer–distancer" marriage pattern is quite common. Usually the pursuing spouse is the wife. Men do not invest enough of themselves or derive enough satisfaction from the marriage. Contrary to "pop psych," men also have needs for intimacy and security. Men experience great distress if the marriage ends, and in approximately 75 percent of cases it is the woman who leaves the marriage. In essence, good marriages are able to tolerate periods of stress or low motivation because the husband and wife approach hard times as an intimate team.

SAMANTHA AND CHARLES

Samantha and Charles' marriage provides an example of a viable, yet imperfect, marriage. Samantha was 44, the custodial parent of two daughters (15 and 13) from her first marriage, which had ended 6 years previously. Charles was 52, and this was his first marriage. They had been married 3 years. Samantha and Charles engaged in marital therapy for a year and continued 6-month follow-up sessions for an additional 2 years. They were committed to their marriage, actively working on it, yet were realistic in recognizing its vulnerabilities and problems.

Charles was the driving force behind the marriage. He came from a family in which the marital model was stable but emotionally distant and, as he later discovered, filled with secrets and anger. In college and young adulthood, Charles' driving force was career success. He was a stockbroker who conscientiously tracked market research and was an excellent salesman. Although he dated and had lovers, his career came first. Charles assumed he would marry and have children, but it was not a high priority.

At 36, Charles had a destructive affair with an emotionally volatile woman. After a night of drinking, he was unable to maintain an erection and she was vitriolic in her denunciations. Rather than walking away from this relationship, Charles became obsessed with proving he was a great lover. The next 2 years were an emotional roller coaster. She wrecked the two cars he gave her, and caused a more lasting impact by destroying his sexual confidence.

During the next 10 years, Charles' life was driven by sexual desperation and embarrassment. He clung to relationships that were unhealthy. He dated younger women hoping that would cure him, went to a self-styled "surrogate," tried penile injections from a urologist, and when Viagra came on the market was hopeful the little blue pill would cure him.

Samantha took pride in being one of the first, and most successful, female actuarials hired by a highly respected company. Samantha married at 29 because family and children were important to her. She had grown tired of the dating scene, and was looking forward to a stable, intimate marriage. Unfortunately her desire to marry overshadowed her judgment about choosing a partner she was comfortable with, attracted to, and trusted. Her first husband met only one of those criteria—attraction. Samantha mistakenly believed opposites attract. He was a surgeon, and she thought someone who had the discipline to get through medical school and a demanding residency would be a stable person. How wrong she was. He was a high-energy risk-taker and a very erratic surgeon. Samantha was proud that she had the courage to leave. The ex-husband remained a source of tension because he was erratic in his visitations and was late or skipped child support payments. The chaos of his life continued to disrupt Samantha's life.

One reason Charles was not accepted by the children was because the ex-spouse made fun of Samantha's second marriage. Charles had none of the charm, biting wit, or charisma of the ex-spouse. The sexual comparison particularly intimidated Charles.

Samantha and Charles entered couple therapy to deal with the erectile dysfunction. Therapy was broad-based—involving stepparenting, work responsibilities, couple friends, extended family, and setting up their new house. Charles was a "pleaser." He would do anything to keep Samantha happy. Samantha enjoyed emotional and financial security but was upset with Charles' passivity. Charles was so afraid of being compared to the biological father that he was a pushover. The children neither respected nor liked him. They were too old for a substitute father.

Charles would never be the sexual partner he could have been. Anticipatory and performance anxiety were too ingrained. Couple sex therapy, including using Cialis as part of their lovemaking, did result in significant improvement. Charles and Samantha developed a pleasure-oriented sexual style. They became comfortable with three types of scenarios: non-demand pleasuring that was intimate and caring, but not erotic; being aroused and orgasmic using manual or oral stimulation; sexual intercourse with Samantha initiating and guiding insertion of his penis. Pleasuring and eroticism became a healthy part of their marriage.

Samantha was more satisfied with their sexual relationship than Charles. He wanted sex to be totally predictable and include intercourse each time. Charles was not satisfied with 85 percent of sexual interactions being good; he wanted 100 percent. There is a natural variability and flexibility to couple sexuality, especially after age 50. Samantha accepted and enjoyed this, Charles continued to fight it. He wanted perfect sexual performance to compensate for the past 20 years. Perfectionism subverts marital and sexual satisfaction.

Samantha accepted this was an imperfect marriage, but realized there were many more strengths than weaknesses. She liked and respected Charles and enjoyed being married to him. She wished they were not burdened by the hassles of the ex-husband and that Charles had a better relationship with her children, but realized these could not be changed. They very much enjoyed their new house. Both were happy and successful in their profession. Their financial status and retirement planning were exceptional, they had couple friends, and shared a variety of interests and activities. Samantha felt she got more out of the marriage than Charles, and wished he were less hard on himself.

Charles valued being married to Samantha. It was a dream come true. He agreed that sex had much improved but still compared himself to what he was before age 35 and to the ex-husband. Charles needed constant reassurance that the marriage was stable and that Samantha was happy. Couple therapy had been of value, but past scars fed unnecessary criticalness and anxiety.

The Limits of Satisfaction

Happily married couples enjoy enhanced life satisfaction, but people in abusive or self-defeating marriages suffer high rates of emotional and health problems. Most second marriages are neither ecstatic nor destructive. The marriage is viable, but imperfect. All marriages (first, second, or subsequent) have areas of dissatisfaction. By its very nature, marriage is not perfect.

How do you decide what problems can be changed and which need to be accepted? What problems are corrosive and could destroy the marriage? There are two major marital myths: that if you truly love your spouse, your marriage will have no problems, and that marriage will solve all personal problems. Marriage cannot and does not bestow self-esteem. Phobias, poor work habits, impulsiveness, alcoholism, cancer, job dissatisfaction, a child who acts out will not go away because of marriage. Marriage is a source of support and motivation in dealing with difficult personal issues, but marriage does not cure them.

Problems and vulnerabilities exist in all individuals and marriages. To believe otherwise is to live in a fairy tale. Which problems can be resolved, which lessened, and which must you learn to accept? Problems that tear at the fabric of the marital bond must be addressed. For example, in the sexuality area, you can increase empathy, communicate better, and feel you are an intimate team. Sexual frequency and pleasure increase. However, the nonorgasmic woman seldom becomes the most sexually desirous and orgasmic woman in the neighborhood. The male with erection or ejaculation problems does not become a "sexual stud." Sexuality becomes functional and the marriage intimate, but sexuality is not the crux of the relationship.

Satisfaction with a second marriage involves realistic expectations. This includes accepting the spouse with weaknesses as well as strengths. It means not expecting this marriage to compensate for the problems and pain of the first marriage. The person who says "if you loved me you would change" is setting herself and the marriage up for failure. Marriage is not about changing yourself to satisfy your spouse. Healthy marriages are based on a positive influence process, where the spouse states feelings and perceptions, makes requests for change and facilitates the change process. You cannot demand or force the spouse to change. Seeing change as a symbol of lovability or worth sets the stage for hurt and anger.

There are limits to change. The person who is compulsive and organized will not become laid back. The spouse who irritates you because she does not balance the checkbook will not suddenly gain the precision of an accountant. The person who is used to spending time with friends and extended family will not be as couple-oriented as the person who prefers one-on-one interactions. You can positively influence your spouse, but you cannot turn her into a different person.

Imperfections and Hard Times in Our Marriage

We enjoy being married and our bond of respect, trust and intimacy has grown over time. We recognize we are not perfect people; nor is our marriage perfect. We are aware of each other's weaknesses and vulnerabilities. That these are accepted and we are still loved and respected makes us feel special and secure.

Barry's lack of mechanical skill, his obvious discomfort in formal situations and clothing, and his boredom if there is not "something on the agenda" are not traits Emily shares or appreciates. Emily's lack of interest and competence in financial matters, feeling intimidated when traveling in exotic locales, and dislike of crowds are characteristics Barry wishes were different. We accept these and work around them. We have good relationships with plumbers and car mechanics, and Barry travels with adult children or by himself to third-world countries.

Surviving hard times is something we are proud of rather than embarrassed by. There have been four prolonged, difficult periods in our marriage. The last, and most difficult, continued for 2 years and was particularly hard for Emily. We look back on these periods and feel angst and regret. We learned from them and hope we will not repeat the same mistakes. Confidence in ourselves, each other, and our relationship has increased. We do not look forward to hard times, but know if we work together we will cope and survive.

There are several problems we grapple with—financial issues, coordinating schedules, difficulty finding new couple friends to whom both of us can relate, different hobbies and interests, different views of religion, disagreements about relationships with adult children. A stylistic difference is that Barry likes to talk out and analyze alternatives while Emily prefers to go with her instincts and self-styled commonsense.

We appreciate areas in which we are in synch, and our lives are enriched by the other's interests. Barry has come to appreciate gardens, quilts, architecture, and small town living because of Emily's influence. Emily has learned to enjoy travel, ethnic restaurants, politics, and different styles of living because of Barry's influence. We value both our similarities and differences.

Exercise—Change and Acceptance

A viable marriage is anchored by acknowledgment of personal attributes, couple strengths, nurturing experiences, and aspects of the spouse and marriage that you value. This exercise addresses negative personal and spousal attributes, unsuccessful or painful experiences, and areas in which you feel hurt, rejected, or angry. Should you deny these, launch a massive personal and couple improvement program, or feel overwhelmed and give up? This exercise explores an alternative way to understand and incorporate negatives into your marriage without feeling guilty or blaming.

Each person develops two lists—negative attributes of the spouse and negative attributes of the marriage. Focus on current issues, not the past. For example, if the spouse had a gambling problem 5 years ago but has not gambled in 3 years, that is not a current issue. What is a current issue, however, is anger over paying accumulated debts.

Personal and couple problems should be stated as clearly and specifically as possible. Negative personal characteristics include a friendship ending because the spouse was uncaring or irresponsible, smoking or insomnia, boredom because of few interests or hobbies, an orgasm or desire problem, low self-esteem, a chronic physical or mental health problem, poor money management, underfunctioning in a career. Examples of couple problems are having three arguments a week, lack of couple friends, feeling unappreciated, being overly dependent, not parenting as a team, having infrequent or low-quality sex, being tense when visiting in-laws, lacking quality couple time.

In examining these lists with your spouse, place each problem into one of two categories: problems you can change and problems you need to accept. For example, the boredom problem could be addressed by enrolling in a continuing-education course by yourself or with your spouse, becoming active in a community group, learning a new sport, volunteering for a worthy cause. The spouse agrees to support and reinforce these changes. Some problems are better addressed by seeking therapy. Entering psychotherapy is not a sign of weakness. Working with a therapist can be the most efficient and effective means of resolving personal or couple problems. (See Appendix A for guidelines when seeking a therapist.)

There are individual and couple negatives that are not changeable or would require too much time and effort. The best strategy is acceptance. An example is the person who is not a good cook or fix-it man and has neither the interest nor skill. Other examples are realizing you will not receive promotions at work, will not be able to afford your dream house, will never achieve the acceptance you would like from your in-laws. Not every personal or couple problem has a solution. Accept negatives without negating yourself or the marriage. Be sure problems do not dominate or become unrealistically important.

Accepting and Valuing the Imperfect Marriage

The ability to survive hard times is a crucial characteristic of a second marriage. Any couple can get along when things are going well and the partners are in love. Couples who cope with difficult situations and survive feel pride. Problems successfully resolved are a cause for celebration. Sad outcomes are accepted. Most important, the couple stays away from the guilt–blame trap. One of the most destructive patterns is keeping score of these failures and angrily demanding retribution.

Intentionality is a crucial concept. You trust that your spouse has your best interest in mind and would not intentionally harm or undercut you. The spouse who is anxious about money verbally chastises his partner for not getting a bonus. His intention is not to put down her competence or contribution but to express worry or frustration. However, the person who uses anger, sex, money, or power to intentionally manipulate and undercut is not someone you want to be married to. The answer is divorce, not trying to understand or reach agreements. When the intention is to harm, the marriage is not viable.

An effective way to stop an escalating power struggle is to focus on the motivations and intentions of each spouse. When you trust that the spouse's intention is to address the issue and not be harmful, it stops the destructive cycle. The discussion can resume on a problem-solving track.

Couples hope they will not have to deal with crises and losses. When these occur, they feel anger and frustration, often aimed at the spouse. Crisis, loss, and hard times are a normal part of the best marriages and the most functional, loving families. Do not devalue yourself or marriage because of this. The challenge is to cope with and resolve problems, if possible. The true test is to support each other during hard times, avoid the blame–guilt cycle, and stop resentments from building. This is easier said than done, especially with chronic problems. If this imperfect marriage is to be viable and satisfying, it is crucial to increase acceptance.

Closing Thoughts

You are not a perfect person, your spouse is not perfect, and this marriage and stepfamily are not perfect. Pop psych books would have you believe that with enough love, insight, prayer, therapy, or willpower you can reach a state of perfection and happiness. It is a seductive, but false, promise. All people, marriages, and families have weaknesses, vulnerabilities, and sadness. That does not mean they are failures. Imperfect marriages are viable and worthwhile. The true test of a second marriage is its ability to survive hard times with the bond of respect, trust, and intimacy intact.

CHAPTER 13

Marriage After 50

People do not expect to be single at 50. The hope is that at this age, you will reap the benefits of the hard work that has gone into your life, marriage, and family. You look forward to stability, grandchildren, and retirement. This is an example of simplistic myths the culture thrusts on us. It is not that this scenario is bad; it just does not reflect reality for many people.

Whether caused by the death of a spouse or breakup of a longstanding marriage, those who are single after 50 face special issues. Throughout this book we emphasize the importance of self-esteem and viewing remarriage as an option, not a mandate. This guideline is particularly relevant after 50.

Demographics concerning divorced or widowed males and females are quite disparate. There are significantly more single females, which increases with age. Males marry younger women (although age roles are becoming less rigid). The majority of divorced or widowed males over 50 do remarry, but the majority of divorced or widowed females over 50 do not remarry. That is the reality. However, statistical averages do not govern individual choices. Women afraid they would never find an available partner do remarry, and female friends are jealous. Two years later when it turns out to be a "caretaker" marriage, she feels stuck and envies the freedom of her single friends. The widowed or divorced man is urged by friends, children, and extended family to remarry because a "man needs a woman." He decides to remain single for three years so he can explore personal and career interests he did not have the time or freedom to engage in when married. When he decides to remarry, it will be for the right reason—to share his life with this woman (not as a substitute for the ex-spouse or for someone to take care of him).

Single by Choice

Although divorce is never easy, it is easier for the person who decided to leave. Divorce is most frequent early in marriage, peaking during the first 4 years. The divorce rate after 12 years is comparatively low. However, divorce does occur then, and with some frequency. The majority of later divorces are initiated by women who conclude that the marriage is getting worse and the spouse will not change. Another pattern is that conflict over adolescents, household tasks, drinking, or financial matters reaches an intolerable level. A third pattern is that one spouse, often the male, becomes involved in a comparison affair and leaves for the lover. A fourth pattern is the partners' lives and interests grow apart, so when they become a "couple again" they discover there is no shared life. Again, it is usually the woman who initiates the divorce in this case.

Being single after 50 often entails a commitment to remain single. Many people enjoy the autonomy of being free from the compromises inherent in being a couple. A common saying is, "Why would I want to pick up someone else's shoes or clean someone's underwear again?"

Friends and extended family provide more emotional support and companionship than the ex-spouse ever did. An example is a divorced woman who observes that although social events are designed with couples in mind, she enjoys dinner parties and outings more than when she was married. It would take a very special man and special relationship for her to consider remarriage. She had to compromise too much of herself in order to keep peace in the marriage. Both profited financially from his over-identification with work, but at great cost to the quality of their lives. She was the primary parent and continues good relations with both adult and adolescent children. She did not reinforce their anger toward the "absent father." The children blame all emotional problems on the father, which she feels negates their personal responsibility. She urges them to deal directly with their father and not use her as the "middleman."

Choosing not to remarry does not mean avoiding relationships. Social and sexual relationships do not require the sanction of marriage. Adults have "sexual friendships" or "lovers." This adds to quality of life as long as the parameters of the relationship are clear to both partners. The danger is trying to make the relationship more than it is. An example is a divorced woman and widowed man who had a lover relationship for 5 years until the man's adult son urged his father to live with her. She reluctantly agreed, but the living together arrangement lasted only four months. Living together caused the relationship to disintegrate. Sometimes people make better friends than lovers; others are better lovers than live-in partners; still others are better living together than being married.

Learning to make healthy relationship decisions is a crucial life skill. This is emphasized with adolescents and young adults but is equally relevant for those over 50. There are many ways to organize one's social and sexual life. Marriage or loneliness are not the only choices; there are a range of healthy alternatives.

The Unwanted Divorce

Some people are single again because of an unexpected, unwanted divorce. It is hard at any age to be rejected, but it is particularly hard for the woman whose husband has left her for an affair or the man whose wife says she can no longer tolerate being married to him. This is a harsh blow to self-esteem. The tendency is to find an immediate salve—drinking, a new love, winning the children to your side. Resist the temptation. The best way to rebuild self-esteem is to focus on yourself. Reinforce healthy activities and relationships and confront unhealthy behaviors and patterns. These changes are for yourself, not to get the ex-spouse to return or to win her approval.

You can learn from the divorce. Accept that this chapter of your life is over. A harmful, yet common, trap is to feel controlled by the ex-spouse's rejection. This is especially true for women who do not remarry. Although it would have been preferable to be married to a man who cared about you and was loyal, you are better off not being married to a man who did not value you and put you down or betrayed you.

A central guideline is that both men and women (especially women) are better being single than trapped in an alienated marriage. Although the divorce might have been unexpected and unwanted, it is a reality. You need to reorganize your life. Divorce can motivate you to make healthy changes. For example, a man stuck in the rut of anger, resentment, and drinking was rudely shocked by the wife's filing for divorce. He could have used the divorce as a reason to be stuck in depression and become a full-blown alcoholic. Instead it served as a wake-up call to retake control of his life. Two years later, he is functioning in a healthy manner. His adolescent children feel they have a father again, although he does not live with them. The ex-wife said that if he had made these changes 2 years before they would still be married. Although they have an amicable relationship, neither has a desire to resurrect the marriage.

Being Widowed

Being widowed is very different than being divorced. People, especially extended family and children, are supportive and there is no stigma. The death of your spouse is a major life stress, especially if there had been a satisfying relationship and the death was unexpected. Even when expected, the death of a spouse is a major loss.

Widowed people are less likely to remarry than those who divorce; this is especially true of women. Widowers are more likely to remarry. The process of grieving and mourning is crucial. Lack of appropriate grieving is a major cause of depression and relationship conflict. Barry's father called the woman he remarried less than a month after his wife died and wanted to marry as soon as possible. They did marry 17 months later (waiting at her insistence). Our family is close to Barry's stepmother. In their 18 years of marriage, she gave a good deal of herself. It was a difficult marriage that might have been easier if Barry's father had spent time grieving and changing himself rather than immediately seeking a wife for companionship and caretaking.

A critical element in rebuilding self-esteem as a widow involves taking personal responsibility. Accepting the reality of death, going through the grieving process, and helping children in their grieving requires time and energy. Practically and emotionally reorganizing your life as a widow is necessary before considering committing to an intimate relationship.

A man with two children under 14 had a wife battling breast cancer. When it became apparent that her condition was terminal, she urged him to remarry for his sake and to give the children a stepmother. He began dating 2 months after her death, but then stopped for a year. He needed to demonstrate to himself (and his children) that he could take care of himself and them. When he remarried it was for an emotional and life partner, not a caretaker. If you remarry for the right reasons, the likelihood of a successful second marriage is much greater. In order to be in that position, you need to develop self-esteem as a single person.

The Alternative to Remarrying

Remarriage is a choice, not a mandate. Contrary to popular myth, some of the happiest, most functional women and men choose to maintain their single status. Let us explore healthy reasons not to remarry. The healthiest reason to remarry is that you have developed a respectful, trusting relationship that includes emotional and sexual attraction. You are committed to sharing your lives. The healthiest reason not to remarry is that you do not have a special person or special relationship. You choose not to settle for a partner you do not love or a relationship with major problems. Other healthy reasons not to remarry include enjoying the freedom and autonomy to manage your life, devoting time to parenting (or grandparenting), focusing on your career, developing a supportive group of friends, volunteering for a community or religious cause, enjoying freedom to travel or adopt an alternative life plan, functioning better as a single person than you did in a marriage.

The chief unhealthy reason for remaining single is fear—fear of rejection, another divorce, and censure from friends or family. Fear-based motivation interferes with psychological well-being. Other unhealthy reasons for remaining single are anger at the opposite sex and/or ex-spouse, fear of intimacy, not wanting to reveal sexual problems, fear of involvements—especially parenting, an excessive need for autonomy, fear that marriage would force you to confront personal problems, dependence on your family of origin, not wanting to give up alimony, a desire to punish the ex-spouse, enjoying sympathy from friends and extended family.

Healthy motivation promotes positive behavior; unhealthy motivation keeps you stuck in self-defeating patterns. Choosing to remain single can be healthy and self-affirming as long as it is motivated by positive, well-thought-out factors. A myth is that people who remain single are afraid of relationships. We recall a 64-year-old friend who divorced when she was 36 and raised four children as a single parent. She maintained strong community and family ties and an active social life. She was involved in her children's lives and considered parenting a prime satisfaction. She was more socially active than her married friends because she had the freedom to pick and choose rather than coordinate with a spouse. She was equally comfortable with single or couple activities, although she preferred group activities. She had romantic/sexual relationships, one which lasted for 6 years. She enjoyed being in a relationship, but would not make life changes (moving, leaving a job, buying a house) for a relationship. If she believed the man would be in her life for a least a year, she involved him with her children. However, she did not give him responsibility or control over the children so that when the relationship ended she did not have to worry about effects on them. Marriage is a major life commitment. Her life was full and satisfying. She never found a man or relationship so positive that she would change her life.

Exercise—Choices in Reorganizing Your Life

Develop self-esteem as a divorced or widowed person. Focus on your self-worth. Decisions based on positive self-esteem are better decisions. Discuss aspects of your life and single status with a respected, trusted friend.

People do not make choices about remarriage in a vacuum. Choosing to remain single or remarry is not an abstract, philosophical decision. It depends on self-esteem and values. Just as important is the situation. Is there a potentially viable relationship? The majority of adults over 50 are desirous of an intimate, secure relationship. However, often there is not an appropriate partner. What do you value and what are you not willing to tolerate in a marriage? Be clear and specific. Being frank with a friend helps you focus.

The next part of the exercise is the most difficult. How can you be sure there will be no negative surprises if you remarry? Will the marriage meet your needs and improve the quality of your life? Not enough time or attention is spent discussing personal vulnerabilities and potential pitfalls. What would present a serious problem for you? How would you react if the man is more interested in a caretaker than a spouse, the partner is not honest about work or financial circumstances, the prospective spouse is responsible for a handicapped adult child he has not told you about, there is a legal judgment against her, he is alienated from an adult child, she wants custody of her grandchildren? Do not keep secrets from the prospective spouse. It is your responsibility to check out sensitive or difficult issues. You do not want devastating surprises.

If you are in a serious relationship, address two topics. Discuss potential issues of difficulty if you were to marry, including sex, finances, children (and grandchildren). In addition, discuss what your life plan is for the next 2 to 5 years. For example, if the person with whom you have a relationship wants to retire in 3 years and move out of state, you are better knowing this up front instead of being surprised after marriage.

Difficult Life Choices

Making a choice is one thing; successfully implementing the choice is quite another. Perhaps the most difficult thing about being single after 50, especially for women, is having a desire to remarry and facing the harsh reality that the type of person and relationship you want is not available. A major trap is marrying for the sake of being married, and feeling stuck in a mediocre or caretaker marriage. A different trap is feeling resentful or worthless because you are not married. Marriage is not necessary for self-esteem. As people stuck in dissatisfying marginal or flawed marriages will tell you, marriage can subvert self-esteem. You desire an intimate, stable marriage. If that is not available, self-esteem and psychological well-being is enhanced by remaining single. The loneliest people are not single; they are married people in an alienated or destructive marriage.

Is it the state of being married or the quality of the relationship that affects psychological well-being? It is the latter, especially for women. Women in fatally flawed or unsatisfactory second marriages feel burdened and have a markedly lower sense of well-being than divorced or widowed women. This is less true for men. Men in satisfying marriages report high psychological well-being. Men in difficult marriages report better functioning than do single or widowed men. This is because single men do not take good care of themselves, especially concerning eating, drinking, sleeping, and health patterns. Marriage provides stability and regularity, which improves the man's functioning, even if it does not make him happy. Contrary to the cultural myth, males need marriage more than females. Males find it easier to tolerate difficult or flawed marriages. Career, sports, politics, and community activities buffer marital dissatisfaction. Males take difficult marriages in stride; they blame themselves less and feel less guilty than do females.

Males over 50 are more likely to remarry than females, and more likely to remarry than younger males. Avoiding loneliness and the need for stability are strong pulls for older men, almost regardless of the quality of the relationship. Males are more likely to turn to a spouse for help than friends, adult children, or extended family. The role of the woman as a caretaker is very powerful, especially for older men. We strongly encourage males to be active, involved partners in their second marriage.

Some men enter second marriages with low expectations and a hidden agenda (wanting to be taken care of, desiring a parent for their children, needing the social acceptability of marriage). Many second marriages end in divorce because the woman is angry at the deception and will not tolerate a low-quality relationship. She would rather be single than in this marriage. The man is shocked and angry because he has lost what he took for granted. We strongly encourage couples to explicitly state what they want and discuss a two- to five-year plan. Too many couples do not get what they expect, and for some there are devastating disappointments. Resentment that the marriage was entered into under false pretenses subverts life satisfaction.

The Role of Adult Children and Grandchildren

In younger marriages, you need to deal with the family of origin. In older marriages, you need to deal with the family of creation— adult children and grandchildren. Marriage is a package deal; you get not just the spouse but his children and grandchildren. Grandchildren are open to a new grandparent, but few adults are looking for a replacement parent. Ideally, you develop a friendship (or at least a cordial relationship) with stepchildren.

Financial fears influence adult children: the new wife will get the house and inheritance. This fear is exacerbated when there is a large age difference (a 67-year-old man marries a 37-year-old woman or a 72-year-old woman marries a 48-year-old man). Although there are marriages with hidden financial agendas or downright scams, the majority of marriages are entered into with the hope for a genuine marital bond. It calms the fears of adult children to explain financial plans to them. The parent has to lead his life in a way that makes sense to him. He wants the help and support of both his new spouse and adult children. He hopes they develop a cooperative, not competitive, relationship.

BILL AND LINDA

Bill, 61 years old, had been married to 39-year-old Linda for 14 months. Four years previously, his ex-spouse had initiated divorce proceedings. It was an emotionally draining divorce for Bill and his three adult children (one of whom had two children of her own). The ex-spouse had returned to work and decided her life would be better single. Bill felt angry, betrayed, and desperate to maintain the marriage. He begged his children to intervene, but two were wise enough not to become involved and one sided with the mother. Conflict over money and the house made the next 2 years the worst of Bill's life. Bill worked for an airline, and one of the most contentious aspects of the divorce is she wanted him to retire so she would have access to the retirement income. Bill's therapist urged him to continue working because work was an area of stability and self-esteem.

Bill did what divorced males do to deal with rejection: He sought a woman who would not reject him. He went through eight relationships before dating Linda. Linda was a single parent of a 9-year-old son. She had not married the father. Linda had previously married and divorced, with no children. Linda helped nurture Bill's psychological health, and Bill provided a stable home for her and her son. Linda was satisfied with the marriage, although she worried about Bill's tendency toward anger and depression.

Linda enjoyed the day-to-day aspects of their life. Bill was an excellent stepfather; the son was thriving under Bill's attention and guidance. The son loved going to the airport and learning the intricacies of flying. Linda quit the full-time secretarial job she hated, and enjoyed the part-time retail job that allowed more parenting and personal time. Linda was the backup babysitter for Bill's daughter, a role she enjoyed. It was strange being a parent and grandparent simultaneously, but Linda relished being with the grandchildren. What she did not enjoy was dealing with Bill's two sons, one of whom was her age and the other 3 years younger. They did not like her, and she found them difficult— especially the bachelor son, who had all of Bill's problematic characteristics but none of his positive ones. Bill tried, unsuccessfully, to be the middleman. Linda had to establish a relationship with each adult child.

Linda enjoyed their townhouse, although Bill missed the spaciousness of the detached house he had to sell. Bill was pleased with his new life and marriage, but continued to resent the ex-spouse and financial losses. He felt awkward about holidays and birthdays; arrangements involving the children and grandchildren were strained. As a friend said, "Bill, you have to accept that life is more complicated when you're divorced." Linda was aware of the age difference and worried how that would affect their lives when he retired. At this point it was not a problem. Bill did not worry about the age difference, seeing it as an energizing force that made him feel younger, especially being involved in Boy Scouts and the son's athletic activities.

Bill resented the divorce, yet was happy with Linda. Linda was glad she had married Bill. There were problems and challenges, especially in dealing with his adult children, but it was a solid marriage. In truth, the marriage was better for Bill than Linda.

RUTH

Ruth was a 59-year-old widow. She had been 57 and married for 26 years when her husband died of a second heart attack 2 years previously. The last 3 years of the marriage had been sad and difficult because he had not been a good patient. Although urged to make major life style changes, he could not successfully implement them. He reduced smoking to ten cigarettes a day, but ate more. He stopped drinking beer, but would not give up his cocktail before dinner. The cardiologist advised an aggressive treatment protocol that Ruth supported, but Frank was not motivated. During the last year, Ruth lived in fear of the eventual heart attack. When he died she was overwhelmed by a range of feelings. Some were expected and accepted, such as sadness, grief, tears, loneliness. Other feelings were confusing and caused shame—anger, relief from worry, freedom from the caretaker role, a sense of independence. Who could she share these feelings with?

Ruth had two adult children. One lived 2,000 miles away, had a wife Ruth did not feel close to, and a grandson she adored. Her divorced daughter lived 30 miles away and had two children. Ruth enjoyed this contact, and the 7-year-old would often stay overnight at grandma's. Most of Ruth's friends were couples. Although her friends were supportive, she realized that her being a widow was uncomfortable for many of them. Her best friend was very supportive, but Ruth worried about disrupting the tenuous state of her friend's marriage by antagonizing the friend's husband. The friend reassured Ruth that she had "done everything she could to care for Frank, and made the last 3 years of his life as good as possible." She acknowledged Ruth's mixed feelings of relief, anger, and freedom.

One of the most helpful suggestions was that Ruth join a 15-session grieving and mourning group. Although the majority of the 12 members were widows, there were also widowers, and parents—one of whom had lost an adult child to AIDS and another who had an adolescent die in a car accident. Although the circumstances were different, the feelings were similar. Ruth appreciated sharing reading material, discussing coping techniques, and realizing that grieving was a normal process. Increasingly, she accepted her feelings. One group member said how much she admired

Ruth. Ruth was referred to a financial advisor. She made good financial and budgeting plans and wrote a will.

A member of the group gave Ruth's name to a single friend. Ruth was flattered, yet intimidated, at being asked on a date for the first time in 28 years. She was pleasant, but firm, saying she was not ready for a serious relationship. Ruth did want a social and sexual life. Fifty-nine was too young to give up men and sex. Over the last 5 years, sex had almost disappeared in the marriage. Marital sex had been traditional, with Frank initiating, and focused on intercourse. Ruth enjoyed sex and was usually orgasmic but wished for more communication and better quality pleasuring. As Frank became ill, erectile functioning became unreliable. Although Ruth was willing to engage in penile stimulation and help him become aroused, he withdrew and avoided sex. With the cessation of intercourse, affectionate and sensual touching almost disappeared. Ruth missed this greatly, just as much as intercourse and orgasm. She masturbated, but felt self-conscious.

Sixteen months after becoming a widow, Ruth went on her first "date." She had ambivalent feelings. She enjoyed going out as part of a couple, being attended to as a woman, and the affection. She was put off by the pressure to be sexual, the assumption she should be grateful to be taken out, the "cute" lines, and her escort's self-centeredness. Ruth decided she would rather do activities in groups or with couple friends than date a man she did not respect. This guideline served her well.

Masturbation was a superior option to a meaningless affair. Ruth remained open to a "lover" relationship. She had offers from married men and was tempted, but decided to date only widowed or divorced men. She had a relationship that lasted 8 months but regretfully broke it off because she could not tolerate his anger when he drank. She had tried to address this three times, but he was not motivated to change. Although there was much she enjoyed about the relationship (including being sexual), she found the anger intolerable.

Ruth has reorganized her life as a widow, and finds much to be satisfied with, including social and community contacts, relationships with children and grandchildren, and having successfully grieved and coped with the death of her husband. She takes satisfaction in managing her finances and investments, enjoys decorating the house, and has a fulfilling 20-hour-a-week volunteer coordinator position. She admits to difficulties, including wishing for a man to accompany her to social events, missing an active sexual life, regretting past choices. She experiences loneliness, especially in the early evening and wishes there were more activities open to single women. Ruth has not ruled out remarriage but has no expectations it will occur and is discerning about whom she becomes involved with.

Asking the Right Questions

Remarriage is a major step. This is even truer after 50. A commitment to share your emotional, practical, sexual, financial, and parenting life is a crucial choice. Marriage has more effect on psychological well-being than any other life component. A vital bond of respect, trust, and intimacy enhances self-esteem and psychological well-being. A destructive or fatally flawed marriage subverts self-esteem and psychological well-being (especially for women).

In one's younger years, there is a personal, family, and cultural push to marry. More than 90 percent of people do marry. However, marriage is not a mandate. Especially after 50, marriage needs to be a well-thought-out choice. Asking the right questions is crucial. Are there positive reasons to marry this person? Socially it is easier to be married, but that is not a healthy reason to marry. Is there a bond of respect, trust, and intimacy and will it be maintained if you join your lives? Have you honestly shared personal and couple strengths and weaknesses? Are there major secrets? Have you discussed issues of money, adult children, sex, and how and where you will live? Do you agree on a 2- to 5-year plan? Have you discussed the hard issues and conflicts that you will face personally, as a couple, and as a stepfamily? There are no guarantees in marriage or life, but confronting hard questions makes it unlikely there will be destabilizing surprises.

Closing Thoughts

Being divorced or widowed after 50 poses special issues. You need to reorganize your life as a single person and ask yourself the right questions about remarriage. Whether out of choice or necessity, you can have self-esteem and a satisfying life as a single person. Remarriage is a choice, not a mandate. Be sure this marriage will meet your needs and is viable. A special trap for women is falling into a "caretaker" marriage. A special trap for men is marrying because of fear of being alone.

Throughout the book our pro-marriage viewpoint is obvious. However, there is little worse in life (especially with aging) than being married to someone you do not respect, trust, or can share intimacy with. The marital bond needs to be strong since you will face personal, couple, financial, health, and sexual issues, as well as challenges dealing with adult children and grandchildren.

CHAPTER 14

Cost-Benefit Assessment
of Difficult Marriages

If you had the courage to leave a fatally flawed first marriage and chose well, how could your second marriage be in trouble? Is it him/me or the institution of marriage?

If this marriage is not meeting your needs, how do you decide whether to divorce, work to improve it, or accept the spouse and marriage for what it is? Can you deal with a second divorce? Statistically, the divorce rate is higher for second marriages, exceeding 60 percent. Partly this is because second marriages have more structural stress such as dealing with a stepfamily and ex-spouse. In addition, the partners know that although divorce is painful, they will survive. People are less tolerant of difficult or marginal second marriages.

What is a difficult marriage? It is a marriage that does not meet realistic goals of respect, trust, and intimacy. It is unrealistic to hope that the spouse will meet all your practical and emotional needs and provide a "golden" life. It is realistic to expect the spouse to respect and trust you, and share emotional and sexual intimacy.

In difficult marriages, there are major deficits in function and feelings. In this chapter, we will guide you in assessing your relationship and deciding whether to continue in the marriage.

Ideally, relationship problems are short term and changeable. What makes a marriage difficult are chronic problems and lack of motivation for change. Examples include a depressed or obsessive–compulsive spouse who will not seek treatment, parenting a disabled child, chronic financial problems, a sexual life that is infrequent or dysfunctional, repeated difficulties with extended family, conflicts over sleeping or eating habits, one or both spouses having affairs, alienation or devitalization, resentment over past conflicts, drug or alcohol abuse, dissatisfaction with living conditions. The pattern of continuous problems devitalizes the relationship and causes chronic dissatisfaction.

People (especially women) read self-help articles and books or listen to talk or call-in shows that offer simple solutions and guaranteed cures. This over-promising approach is seldom true. The reality is that these are powerful, deeply ingrained patterns that are difficult to change, much less totally cure. Working to reduce problems and achieving meaningful change is healthy; hoping for miracle cures is unhealthy and adds to dissatisfaction and resentment. Hope is not enough. You have to commit to the change process, use appropriate helper resources, put time and energy into a change plan, and maintain motivation long enough to obtain significant (although non-perfect) improvement.

The Choice Process

There are three basic strategies: leave the marriage, work to improve it, or accept the spouse and marriage for what it is. It takes two people to remain married, but only one person to divorce. Seldom is the decision to separate mutual. The person who desires the marriage and believes in its viability is stuck with the unfairness. The harsh reality is that one person cannot maintain a marriage.

The decision to divorce is seldom rational or planned. It is very difficult to sit with a spouse and intellectually tick off the reasons you do not want to remain married. Most marriages end in an emotionally explosive manner. This is unnecessary and harmful, but understandable. Separation occurs when one person feels that the marriage is not viable and gives up hope for change.

We suggest that this decision be thought out and discussed with a respected confidante or professional, not made on the basis of impulse or emotion. Once a marital bond is broken, it is very difficult to reverse the process.

The usual guideline is to make a good faith couple commitment of at least 6 months to change the personal and/or marital problems. The realistic goal is significant, meaningful change, not a total cure. For example, a spouse with anxiety or obsessive–compulsive problems is unlikely to make a total reversal and be laid back. A reasonable expectation is that the compulsive behavior can be significantly reduced so it minimally disrupts the marriage. There are still irritants (anxiety about driving on a superhighway or fastidiousness about everything being in place), but the problems are no longer controlling.

There are some behaviors that are intolerable even if infrequent, such as driving drunk, physical abuse, suicidal or homicidal actions, or child abuse. Most problems are on a continuum of acceptability. The spouse has to be clear about what behavior is unacceptable, what is tolerable although difficult, and what constitutes a healthy change. Supporting and acknowledging change while accepting the remaining problems is the most common outcome.

The third strategy is to accept the chronic difficulties for what they are, detach from the problems but not from the person, and focus on what is valuable in the marriage. This strategy emphasizes acceptance. Rather than focus on what is problematic and unchangeable, the partners focus on what is satisfying and enjoyable. An example is a spouse who has mild organic impairment from a head injury that results in his unemployability. However, he is a good parent, companion, and householder. This is not what his wife planned or hoped, but she accepts this and enjoys its compensations, which include freedom to pursue her career. The key is to not fall into resentment or alienation. Many marriages become devitalized, and the couple stays together but is resentful. There must be genuine detachment and acceptance of problems by the partners while actively enjoying the positives of their lives and marriage.

The Stigma of a Second Divorce

A second divorce carries the stigma a first divorce had a generation ago. This is unfair, but true. Divorce is a choice that should not be stigmatized. You are better divorced than in a destructive marriage. This is true whether it is a first, second, or third divorce. A second divorce leaves you vulnerable to a special set of personal and cultural stresses. An especially difficult question is whether the children should maintain contact with the former stepparent. Although there is no legal bond, there is often an emotional bond. Ultimately, it is the biological parent's decision. This should be based on the best interests of the child, not the parent's feelings about the ex-spouse. Dealing with two ex-spouses, especially if children are involved, multiplies the complications. That reality needs to be confronted, not ignored.

The most important factor is rebuilding self-esteem. No one plans to be divorced a second time. A man divorced his wife when she was arrested for an insurance scam. His parents urged him to support her through this crisis, especially since they had a child and she had been an involved stepparent for his two children from the first marriage. He felt she had violated a trust and would not maintain a life free of scams. He was not defensive about this decision. He had done the hard but right thing. In reorganizing his life, he had to deal with financial and legal realities, as well as psychological and parenting issues. He retained a lawyer to limit his legal liability during the separation and divorce process.

How does one deal with extended family and religious and community pressures? Be prepared for some family members and friends to be judgmental or break off contact. That is unfortunate, but you need not be shameful about this. It is their decision and their loss. It is not in your best interest to try to convince them that the divorce is okay or win them back. Remarried friends avoid you because they fear a "contagion effect." Again, it is their decision and their loss. People develop friendships with those whose life is similarly organized. You benefit from friendships with people who share and support your life situation. You and the children need family, social, religious, and community support.

How can you help the children deal with the reactions of others? It is not healthy for a child to apologize for her family. The child has worth; her healthy development is a priority, and she should not elicit or accept pity from others. She should be encouraged to acknowledge family strengths as well as problems and be aware of the diversity of families. The traditional nuclear family is not the only good type of family. Help the child respond to questions and teasing. The parent should encourage her to ask questions and discuss concerns. It is crucial to be an "askable parent."

Crises vs. Chronic Problems

The adage that crises provide a challenge from which people can learn and grow is too pat, but it does contain a great deal of truth. People do not like crises, but if successfully resolved they can be sources of pride. It is not the crisis that tears the marriage apart but how the crisis is handled. For example, if a spouse is given a choice to relocate or be laid off, this throws the marriage and stepfamily into crisis. For the couple who considers alternatives and reaches a mutual decision, it can strengthen the marriage and improve the family's financial and living situation. However, if it results in multiple job changes and moves it is demoralizing and becomes a chronic problem.

Couples can survive financial problems, but only if both partners deal with the situation and each other responsibly. The spouse who stops looking for work puts the marriage in jeopardy. The spouse who is not honest about money or misuses credit cards also puts the marriage in danger. The more difficult and chronic the problem, the greater the need for communication and the couple to work as a team. Ignoring or blaming leads to a conflicted, devitalized marriage that is ripe for divorce.

Chronic problems not involving the couple's relationship—dealing with an underachieving child, a parent suffering from Alzheimer's, a business that is marginal, deterioration of the neighborhood—requires adopting a coping strategy so the problem does not dominate the marriage. For example, devote an evening a week to sorting out medical, social service, financial, practical, and emotional issues involving the ill parent. Unless there is an emergency or a decision has to be made immediately, wait for the appointed evening to discuss a demoralizing, chronic problem.

Chronic personal or relationship problems raise difficult issues. A spouse who is chronically depressed, has a serious health problem but will not stop smoking, continues to obsess about a business failure, is angry and vindictive toward an in-law, refuses to take responsibility for financial problems engenders animosity and resentment. The person is "stuck," and the spouse runs out of patience. Examples of chronic couple problems include a pattern of once-a-week bitter

arguments, being sexual less than twice a month, one spouse insist-
ing on having people to the house each weekend when the other
wants time as a couple, holding a grudge against an adult child,
maintaining an extramarital affair, continuing to support a cause or
church to which the spouse is opposed. Chronic problems devitalize
your relationship and rob it of emotional satisfaction. The marriage
is in a constant state of stress and dissatisfaction.

Threats to Leave

One of the most unsettling things about difficult relationships
is intermittent, emotionally intense threats to end the marriage.
One couple engaged in a year of marital therapy made significant gains, although their marriage remains difficult with chronic
problems. The main change was stopping threats to dissolve the
marriage. They learned productive ways to discuss difficult issues
and avoid use of counterproductive threats. Barry tells couples
that "you can't keep going to the mats." The specter of divorce
dominates the relationship and threats to leave control their lives.
Threats of separation without a behavioral follow-up become hollow but remain a source of resentment and alienation. Threats
are impulsive and emotional, met by anger and counterthreats. It
becomes a "game of chicken."

The guideline is to refrain from separation or divorce threats,
especially in the context of impulsivity. If a spouse is seriously
thinking of separating, she is advised not to state this for at least a
week. She should be sure that this is a motivated, intentional act
and assess how committed she is to separate, and whether she has
a specific plan. The partners should schedule a time to discuss
the state of the marriage. She should disclose how seriously she
is considering leaving, how specific the plans are, how committed
she is to the plan, and what response she wants from her spouse.
This is a vastly different process than impulsive, emotional threats.
Threats and ultimatums—i.e., "going to the mats"— makes a difficult marriage worse. This behavior elicits much drama but promotes no awareness or resolution.

The Need for Resolution

Living with constant, active ambivalence is draining. There is a
need for resolution—whether it involves separation, change, or

acceptance. The resolution can be time-limited or open-ended. Some couples decide on a 6-month structured separation to see how each person functions alone.

Couples with a pattern of separating and reconciling, whether or not they actually live apart, find that marital conflict dominates their lives. Children complain that their practical and emotional needs are ignored because the parents are so consumed by conflict they do not have time or energy for parenting (this can also be true of job, friendships, and community involvements). Rather than the marriage accounting for one-quarter of self-esteem, it becomes the overwhelming, controlling life issue. These couples can benefit from therapy. A primary intervention is an agreement not to separate or threaten separation for a given time (i.e., six months). The couple needs to focus on what changes are desired and what is acceptable (or at least tolerable).

Explore change and acceptance dimensions to increase understanding of your spouse and the relationship. This allows you to assess your needs, those of your spouse, the quality of the relationship, and the strengths and deficits of the individuals and the marriage.

Intolerable Marriages

When discussing first or second divorces, we advocate making a decision based on an assessment of practical, emotional, parental, financial, and psychological factors. The decision to remain married is not a moral issue (i.e., staying married is not the right choice, getting divorced is not evil). It is a personal commitment.

Some marriages are destructive and intolerable. Examples include spouse abuse, physical or sexual abuse of children, being hateful, purposefully undercutting the spouse, breaking trust (putting the spouse at risk for HIV or engaging in drug trafficking), stealing or misusing couple funds, living with a spouse addicted to alcohol or drugs. If you remain in a destructive marriage, be clear about your motivations. Consult a professional as to whether this is a healthy decision for you and the children.

A marriage that is destructive to self-esteem, life, or family is not worth maintaining. Providing a safe and nurturing, environment for children is more important than clinging to an abusive marriage. Some marriages are fatally flawed, and good intentions, therapy, prayer, or hope will not make them tolerable. Confront the harsh reality that this is a destructive marriage. Divorce is the healthy option.

JILL AND ADAM

Jill was in a second marriage of 8 years to Adam (his first marriage). Jill was the custodial parent of a 14-year-old son and 12-year-old daughter. Together, they had twins, who were 6 years old when she had a tubal ligation. Jill was 35 and Adam 37.

Jill and Adam had a pattern of twice-a-week arguments that degenerated into physically abusive incidents with a frequency of once or twice a month. Both engaged in the verbal and physical incidents. Jill was more likely to throw things and hit Adam with objects (i.e., a chair). Adam would hit her on the face and upper body. During and after these incidents, threats of divorce or actually leaving for a day were common.

The couple sought marriage counseling from a pastoral counselor and engaged in a church-sponsored couple communication and anger-expression weekend workshop. Although some techniques and exercises were helpful, the usual outcome was that they felt confused and frustrated. They entered therapy with a marriage therapist. The therapeutic contract was to make a six-month good faith effort to rebuild a viable marriage. During this period, Jill and Adam agreed not to make any threats of separation.

The first issue was to eliminate abusive incidents and reduce the frequency and intensity of arguments. Adam and Jill needed to stop the "poison." Physical incidents ceased, although verbal arguments continued. The most significant change was improved parenting, especially with the twins. They had a week's vacation as a couple, and discovered they enjoyed being together and sharing sexuality. The quality of their lives and marriage significantly improved.

Jill began to trust Adam and discuss hopes and goals. She wanted to focus on her career and return to work full time. In addition to moving to a new house or renovating the house they lived in, Jill also wanted Adam to be an involved stepparent. When Jill asked what Adam wanted, she was bitterly disappointed. Adam wanted things to remain status quo. He could tolerate the stepchildren but had no desire to form a closer relationship and planned to increase his activity in the sailing group, which meant he would be gone for several weekends. The therapist observed that these reflected quite discrepant personal styles and values.

Adam raised the issue about which he was most adamant—finances. He was extremely upset by the amount of money Jill spent on the children and house. He insisted that when she returned to full-time work the additional money should go into a retirement account. The therapist intervened when they began exchanging charges of being a "cheapskate" and "spendthrift." Money issues—either income or expenditure—are a major cause of marital conflict.

Jill and Adam were given written and discussion exercises to clarify financial issues and find common ground. Looking at the figures, discussing values, and examining alternatives highlighted the vast gulf. Jill and Adam's life goals, desires for the marriage, relationships with children, and their views on financial matters were very different. This was exacerbated when Adam went on a 2-week sail. It was the highlight of his year and, as Adam pointed out, an inexpensive way to vacation. Jill asked about the family getting involved in sailing, but Adam said that was not feasible. In truth, it was not appealing. Adam would rather sail with the club, many of whose members were divorced. Jill wondered if Adam were interested in one of the women.

With the heat of physical abuse and threats removed, the light was shining clearly on relationship issues. The proverbial "straw that broke the camel's back" occurred during the Christmas holidays. Jill wanted the children to feel close to grandparents, aunts and uncles, and cousins. Adam traveled to her parents but was grumpy. He left the day after Christmas to return to work. Jill later learned there was a planning meeting and party for the sailing club.

Adam announced he was going sailing for a week in the Caribbean. Jill objected, but Adam said since he worked hard and made more money he had a right to vacation where and how he pleased. The basic discrepancy in what each spouse valued had to be accepted or the marriage would not be viable. Jill felt emotionally abandoned but said she would remain married for the sake of the children (a questionable rationale). It was Adam who made the break. He told Jill he was entering a business deal with three members of the sailing club, including the woman he was attracted to.

Although it was not said, Jill suspected there was or would be an affair shortly. Six weeks after Jill and Adam separated, he moved in with this woman.

Jill experienced a range of feelings during the termination of her second marriage. There were the expected feelings of anger toward Adam and the woman, feelings of rejection, stigma about a second divorce, concern for parenting (especially the twins), issues of money and career, and the legal ramifications. Yet, Jill was feeling better than she expected. She had given a good faith effort to salvage the marriage. Although one part of her wished it was she who had said the marriage was over, as the lawyer observed, Jill was in a better negotiating position since Adam had moved in with another woman. Jill would prefer to be single than trapped in a lonely marriage with a spouse who would rather be sailing. Jill continued individual therapy and joined a support group of divorced women with children. She did not look forward to being divorced, but knew she would survive. Jill was dedicated to reorganizing her life as a single person.

Six months after Adam separated, he obtained a vasectomy. He maintained child support payments and monthly visitation, but admitted that parenting was difficult. Organizing his life around work and sailing made Adam a happier person. He declined the opportunity for further therapy, although he felt couple therapy had made it easier to communicate about parenting the twins. Adam liked Jill better after they were divorced. He told the children that their mother was a wonderful person (although not someone to whom he wanted to be married). Jill and Adam lived very different lives post-divorce, but wished each other well and dealt amicably about parenting issues. Jill wished Adam were more involved, but accepted his parenting preference. He has no contact with the stepchildren. Adam maintained financial responsibilities and appreciated the care and concern Jill showed. They were able to stay out of each other's lives and focus on their own.

Living With Your Decision

Once a decision is made, each spouse must be able to live with and accept it, even though it is not ideal or what was hoped for. Perfect resolutions are for novels, movies, and "feel good" books, not real people in difficult marriages. The partners who choose to maintain their marriage can enjoy positive characteristics while accepting difficulties and problems without resentment or bitterness. Choosing means finding peace and serenity in the resolution, being able to let go, and accepting the reality. For example, a husband wanted his wife to resume her career as an attorney. She hated being a lawyer, deriving satisfaction from the less lucrative position as a music teacher. A woman had to accept that her husband underwent periodic depressions that he could alleviate with medication, although this pattern did stress the marriage and family. Every person, marriage, and family has its "Achilles heel" that needs to be monitored and coped with.

Can people feel worthwhile and lovable in difficult marriages? Absolutely yes. You do not need perfection to be in a stable, satisfactory marriage; just make sure the problems do not dominate your life. Couples can and do value difficult marriages. The spouse does not have to be problem-free for you to love him. Stepfamilies with multiple problems not only survive but appreciate the emotional support and practical help they receive despite the problems.

Many couples find that their marriage thrives after the children leave home. Grandparenting is one of the rewards for staying together through hard times. Couples who have weathered problems admit that although they often thought of "throwing in the towel" the fact that they did not threaten this at each crisis was a relief. Knowing there would be good times was of great help. The intimate bond was frayed, but it held.

Exercise—A Cost-Benefit Analysis of a Difficult Marriage

We suggest that you do this exercise in writing, separately from your spouse, and as comprehensively as possible. Each person honestly assesses his/her attitudes, values, and feelings about difficulties with the spouse and marriage. We suggest that this list not be shared now or later. If you know it will be shared, you are less likely to be frank.

Start by listing positive personal characteristics, relationship strengths, practical and financial factors, and parenting strengths. Then focus on difficult characteristics of your spouse and the relationship. Differentiate between acute and chronic problems. Divide the difficulties and problems into three categories: 1) those that are intolerable, 2) those you believe can be changed, and 3) those you can accept. When working on the first category (which most threatens the marriage), be clear about what needs to change to make the situation tolerable. What reductions in frequency and intensity are necessary? What aspect of your spouse's behavior makes it intolerable? Which couple problems are intolerable and why? Have you told this to your spouse? Have either of you tried to change? How motivated are you to maintain the marriage?

Areas of change need to be carefully considered. Good intentions are not enough. You need a specific plan to which you both are committed. A system is necessary to implement and monitor changes. A perfect process or outcome is unlikely; the goal is meaningful change. Seldom do problem areas become strengths. How much of the change process is your responsibility, your spouse's, or a joint responsibility? Do you care enough about your marriage to devote time and energy to implement changes? The major impediment to change is losing motivation and focus.

The second phase is a discussion about this marriage. Are you committed to improving the marriage? Would therapy be helpful? This is our usual suggestion. Consulting a professional is a powerful resource to help maintain motivation and facilitate the change process. If you decide to try on your own, be sure to keep lines of communication open and work together. As you focus on problems, do not forget individual and couple strengths that make this marriage worthwhile, even with its difficulties.

If one or both spouses decides the marriage is intolerable and wants to separate, they are faced with a different set of issues. The question is how to divorce in the least harmful way, reorganize their lives, and maintain financial and parental responsibilities. We suggest either divorce therapy or divorce mediation to help in this difficult process. Although a second divorce is easier because the partners know what to expect, it is still a stressful process for them and the children.

Re-Organizing Your Life After Your Second Divorce

A major reason that second marriages have a higher divorce rate is that the person is less likely to tolerate a difficult spouse and marriage. Divorce is never an easy choice, but if that is the decision, it needs to be honored, not stigmatized. We encourage individual or group therapy to rebuild self-esteem. When children and stepchildren are involved, family therapy should be considered.

There is no logical reason for greater stigma over second than first divorces. If the marriage is abusive or destructive, it is not worth preserving. Do not naively expect things to fall into place quickly or easily. Friendships need to be rebuilt, and some will not survive. Helping children redefine their relationship with an ex-spouse is complex and difficult. Most divorced stepparents do not keep contact with their stepchildren. That needs to be accepted as a reality, not a reflection on the value of the child. Children need accurate information, specific guidance, and feedback to understand what is happening. Most of all they need permission to express feelings and be listened to in a respectful, caring manner. Children survive divorce and can learn important lessons about autonomy, coping, and adaptability. They can avoid traps of blaming, anger, guilt, or cynicism.

One component in rebuilding self-esteem is a new relationship. The most important guideline is that you realize your personal worth whether in a relationship or not. Avoid intimate relationships for at least three months and up to a year after separating. You have enough to deal with. A romantic relationship distracts your focus. People seek relationships for validation after separation, which is not a healthy motivation. These relationships are more likely to drain self-esteem than to build it.

Closing Thoughts

Realizing you are dealing with a difficult spouse and/or difficult marriage is not a happy discovery. The hope was that the second marriage would be healthy, satisfying, and stable. However, the reality of the difficult marriage must be addressed.

You need to make a wise decision when considering whether to leave the marriage, work to improve it, or accept its difficulties because the pluses outweigh the negatives. Wise decisions consider both emotional and practical factors and short- and long-term effects. This decision is based on your best interests and the best interests of your children and stepfamily. It cannot be based on fears or stigma surrounding a second divorce.

CHAPTER 15

Pride and Acceptance

In reading drafts of this book, friends pointed out a striking paradox. They know that personally and clinically we have a pro-marriage, pro-family bias. They also know we are respectful of divorced people, second marriages, stepfamilies, and individual differences. The paradox is that few writers or clinicians are both pro-marriage and pro-divorce. What ties this together is our advocacy of relationships that enhance self-esteem and psychological well-being. Ideally, a marriage meets needs for intimacy and security. A viable marital bond of respect, trust, and intimacy deserves to be cherished and nurtured. A marriage that subverts self-esteem is destructive, and the decision to divorce is healthy. The fact that the majority of people remarry is a sign they have not given up on marriage but on that fatally flawed marriage.

Many people blame America's high divorce rate on rampant individualism, lack of tradition, loss of respect for the family, or not caring for the children. Our culture's divorce rate is too high. The remedy is better thought-out marital choices, promoting the attitudes and skills that build healthy marriages, and putting emphasis on keeping the marriage vital, satisfying, and committed.

It does not do any good to increase the stigma of divorce or make divorce more aversive. Cultures that prohibit divorce do not promote healthy marriages or families. The anti-divorce movement props up marginal and destructive relationships. It is better to grow up in a single-parent home or amid a stepfamily that promotes healthy relationships than in a dysfunctional nuclear family mired in a non-respectful, non-trusting, non-intimate marriage.

Staying together for the sake of appearances, for religious reasons, or for convenience is not healthy. If the husband–wife relationship is fundamentally troubled, it impacts the entire family, including children. Divorce is the reasonable option. Divorce is not optimal, but in these circumstances divorce is the sensible resolution. A successful second marriage and stepfamily is the optimal follow-up. Maintaining self-esteem as a single person while staying involved as a parent is another healthy resolution.

The reality of the persons involved and their situation is more important than our guidelines. That is one reason for the complex messages. The individuals and the reality of their life together take precedence over theory.

You can enjoy psychological well-being without being married. This book has focused on the challenges and traps of second marriages, but it is perfectly normal to choose not to remarry. Remarriage is not a mandate. Single and divorced people have higher self-esteem than those in dysfunctional marriages (whether a first or second marriage).

Readers and colleagues question whether we over-promote second or subsequent marriages. If second marriages can be successful, why not first marriages? We are not dismissing first marriages; ours is a first marriage. However, many first marriages are fatally flawed—she married the wrong person for the wrong reasons. When the marital bond of respect, trust, and intimacy is broken, it is very difficult to resurrect. Traditionally, couples stayed married regardless of the quality of the relationship, its effect on self-esteem, or problems with children. In the past, societal, religious, and family pressures, along with the stigma of divorce, resulted in dysfunctional but stable marriages. Now marriages have to be of better quality to endure. Promoting strong, viable marriages is a healthy trend for both first and subsequent marriages.

Remarriage does not offer perfect happiness or compensate for the pain of the first marriage. The second marriage should not be burdened with making up for the past. It stands on its own. The bond of respect, trust, and intimacy needs to be strong because of the extra stress of stepfamilies, the ex-spouse, and the higher divorce rate.

Dealing With Reality

One measure of psychological health is the ability to deal with reality rather than deny problems and pretend everything is perfect. Examining past relationships and experiences increases awareness so you do not repeat the same mistakes. Life is meant to be lived in the present rather than feeling guilty or shameful about the past. A value of examining the past is that it empowers you to choose well and enhances a committed marriage in the present. Divorce need not define self-esteem, but it is an integral part of your reality.

"Politically correct family values" denigrate divorce and treat stepfamilies as second class. We advocate acceptance of divorce, remarriage, and stepfamilies. Diversity in families is the reality; there is not "one right way" to be a family. Second marriages and stepfamilies deserve the acceptance and support of extended family, religious groups, the community, and the legal system.

Promotion of Second Marriages

Statistics about second marriages contain a built-in paradox. Couples who establish successful second marriages report greater satisfaction than those in first marriages. Yet, the divorce rate is higher. Second marriages require more thought, effort, and commitment. The second marriage can crumble under the stresses of dealing with the ex-spouse and stepfamily. Second marriages require nurturing and the willingness to deal with differences and problems.

Pride in a successful second marriage is high. A client told Barry, "This time I'm married to my intimate friend and trust we'll support each other through hard times. I want my children to see the love and happiness marriage can bring." In addition to pride, a satisfying, stable second marriage also rebuilds self-esteem. You have accomplished what you set out to do—ended a flawed marriage, learned about yourself and relationships, chose well, and committed the time and effort needed to develop a respectful, trusting, intimate marital bond. The marriage need not be perfect or compensate for the hurt and disappointment of the previous marriage. You feel loved for yourself, for your strengths as well as vulnerabilities.

Pride in the Stepfamily

Stepfamilies are different from nuclear families; they are more complex and have the potential for more problems. Not only do stepfamilies function; many thrive and produce flexible, resilient adults. It helps neither the adults nor children to apologize or be defensive about divorce and stepfamilies. Psychological well-being is promoted by accepting reality, making a commitment to learn from mistakes, doing your best to deal with difficulties, and taking pride in yourself and your family. Stepfamilies are not second class.

Stepfamilies provide children with different parenting models, which can be both problematic and valuable. Adults who grew up in stepfamilies report they are more aware, flexible, and better able to negotiate relationships than peers from nuclear families. They see themselves as more realistic, less tied to conventional patterns, more open to change. These are valuable learnings.

The Importance of Healthy Relationships

There are legitimate "negative glues" that promote marriage: security, social desirability, convenience, community and family support, religious sanctions, economic factors, a two-parent family. These are worthwhile, but they cannot compensate for an angry, destructive marriage. To be viable, the marriage must be healthy and supportive.

The quality of the marriage is very important. Whether it is a first, second, or third marriage, a relationship that meets needs for intimacy and security is of great value. A viable, intimate marriage is a major contributor to a satisfying life.

Quality relationships include individual friends, extended family, work friends, neighborhood friends, other families, as well as friends who share hobbies, community activities, sports, or religious observance. Some couples hide behind the marriage, ignoring other relationships. A positive effect of going through a divorce is to realize the importance of friendships, a social support network, and family relationships. After remarriage, people continue to value individual and couple friendships.

A satisfying second marriage promotes other healthy relationships, especially couple friends. Friendships where you are liked as individuals and a couple are special. Friends who care about your marriage and stepfamily are an important, valuable resource.

Social relationships are particularly important for people who chose to remain single or are single because they do not find a person they want to marry. Same-sex divorced or widowed friends are especially helpful. Having friends who understand and share your life situation is valuable.

First Marriage for One, Second Marriage for the Other

The traditional advice was not to marry a divorced person. The "old wives' tale" was that divorced people were bad marital risks—a simplistic and misleading generalization. There is a special dynamic that exists in a first marriage for one partner and a second (or third) for the other. The naïve optimism that energizes first marriages is not present. The divorced spouse approaches the marriage with a stronger commitment to make it work.

The person marrying for the first time can feel cheated of the joys and optimism. He resents dealing with the ex-spouse and problems and sensitivities not of his making. If these and other issues are not discussed and worked through, misunderstandings and resentments build. Silent disappointments and anger fester and undermine this marriage.

There is a tendency toward "what-if" thinking. "What if we met 5 years ago?" "What if he hadn't been married before?" "What if this marriage doesn't work?" "What if the child doesn't accept the stepfather?" What-if thinking makes for interesting philosophical discussions and bar talk but is not helpful for the second marriage or stepfamily. One spouse was previously married, but that should not be a source of embarrassment or guilt. Nor should it play a dominant role in the dynamics of this marriage. Being divorced does not make the spouse a better or worse person.

Self-Esteem, Psychological Well-Being, and Divorce

Psychological well-being is a central concept that includes self-esteem, quality relationships, competence and achievements, coping with crisis and loss, and a sense of meaning and values. A healthy, viable marriage enhances life satisfaction.

The person who divorces for the right reasons has better self-esteem than the person who stays married for the wrong reasons. The right reasons for divorce include the failure of serious discussions and attempts to revitalize the marriage (including therapy), realization of a fatal flaw, lack of emotional or sexual intimacy, abuse or violence involving the spouse or children, and lack of respect or trust. Divorcing for the right reasons helps rebuild self-esteem.

Closing Thoughts

Divorce is optimal for the person with a destructive or fatally flawed marriage. Being single is both a challenge and an opportunity. If you decide to remarry, be sure it is for healthy reasons, that you have learned from the divorce, and have chosen well. A second marriage and stepfamily provide challenges. If you can successfully meet these challenges, this marriage will enhance self-esteem and offer a fulfilling life.

We hope the information, guidelines, exercises, and case studies in this book have helped you understand, accept, and move beyond your divorce. Take pride in making a difficult decision and acting on it. If you choose to remarry and establish a stepfamily, use all your resources and learnings to be successful. Enjoy this marriage and devote the time and effort needed to keep your marriage vital, satisfying, and stable.

APPENDIX A

Choosing an Individual, Couple, or Family Therapist

As stated in the first chapter, this is not a "do-it-yourself therapy" book. People are reluctant to consult a therapist, feeling that to do so is a sign of "craziness," a confession of inadequacy, or an admission that your life and marriage are in dire straits. In reality, seeking professional help is a sign of psychological wisdom and strength. Entering individual, marital, or family therapy means you realize there is a problem and you have made a commitment to resolve the issues and promote individual, couple, and family growth.

The mental health field can be confusing. Individual, couple and family therapy are clinical subspecialties. They are offered by several groups of professionals including psychologists, social workers, marriage therapists, family therapists, psychiatrists, and pastoral counselors. The professional background of the practitioner is of less importance than his or her competence in dealing with your specific problems.

Some people have health insurance that provides coverage for mental health and thus can afford the services of a private practitioner. Those who do not have the financial resources or insurance could consider a city or county mental health clinic, a university or medical school outpatient mental health clinic, or a family services center. Clinics usually have a sliding fee scale (i.e., the fee is based on your ability to pay).

When choosing a therapist, be assertive in asking about credentials and areas of expertise. Ask the clinician what the focus of the therapy will be, how long therapy can be expected to last, and whether the emphasis is on individual, communication, parenting, relationship, conflict resolution, or sexuality issues. Be especially diligent in questioning credentials, such as university degrees and licensing. Be wary of people who call themselves personal counselors, marriage counselors, or family counselors. There are poorly qualified persons—and some outright quacks—in any field.

One of the best resources for obtaining a referral is to call a local organization such as a psychological association, marriage and family therapy association, or mental health clinic. You can ask for a referral from a family physician, minister, or trusted friend. For a marriage or family therapist, check the Internet site for the American Association of Marriage and Family Therapy at www.Therapistlocator.net.

Feel free to talk with two or three therapists before deciding on one with whom to work. Be aware of comfort with the therapist, degree of rapport, and whether the therapist's assessment of the problem and approach to treatment make sense to you. Once you begin, give therapy a chance to be helpful. There are few miracle cures. Change requires commitment and is a gradual and often difficult process. Although some people benefit from short-term therapy (fewer than ten sessions), most find the therapeutic process will require 4 months to a year or longer.

The role of the therapist is that of a consultant rather than a decision maker. Therapy requires effort, both in the session and at home. Therapy helps to change attitudes, behavior, and feelings. Do not be afraid to seek professional help to assist you in assessing and changing individual, marital, or family problems.

Marriage and Stepfamily Support Groups and Enhancement Programs

Many couples find a marital or stepfamily support group or educational program more acceptable and inviting than professional therapy. Educational programs for couples help you learn attitudes and skills that promote a healthy marriage by learning communication, conflict resolution, and intimacy and sexuality skills in order to build a solid marital foundation. These programs explore normal developmental phases of marriage such as the transition from romantic love/passionate sex to developing an intimate, interactive couple sexual style; the transition from idealizing your spouse and hoping this marriage will compensate for the pain of the first marriage to accepting vulnerabilities and weaknesses as well as strengths and positive characteristics; the transition from being single again to managing time and finances as you balance your marriage and stepfamily; and special issues in forming a stepfamily and talking about roles and expectations.

There are a growing number of resources for remarried couples and stepfamilies ranging from church-sponsored free weekend seminars to a 4-month marital training class sponsored by a fee-based marital enhancement program. An excellent resource for finding a program that could meet your needs is on the internet at smartmarriages.com. There is a directory of training programs, classes and groups for couples and families. The two major organizations focused specifically on second marriages and stepfamilies are the Step Family Association of American at SAAfamilies.org and Stepfamily Organization at stepfamilies.org. These organizations list resources including recommended books and tapes.

The largest sponsors of marital enhancement and second marriage programs are religious organizations. Many of these programs are inexpensive or even free. There are also community organizations, including community college programs, adult education classes, and a variety of practitioners that sponsor programs and support groups for healthy marriages and stepfamilies. We hope these offerings will increase in the future as awareness grows for the need to promote satisfying, stable second marriages and stepfamilies.

APPENDIX C

Recommended Books

Ahrons Constance R. (1998). The Good Divorce. New York: Harper Paperback.

Christensen, Andrew & Jacobson, Neil (2000). Reconcilable Differences. New York: Guilford Press.

Deal, Ron (2002). The Smart Stepfamily. Minneapolis, Minn.: Bethany House.

Scott, Virginia, Doub, George & Rummels, Peggy (1999). Raising a Loving Family. Holbrook, Mass.: Adams Media.

Fisher, Bruce & Albenti, Robert (1999). Rebuilding: When Your Relationship Ends. San Lius Obispo, Calif.: Impact Publishers.

Fowers, Blaine (2000). Beyond the Myth of Marital Happiness. San Francisco, Calif.: Jossey-Bass.

Glass, Shirley (2003). Not "Just Friends". New York: Free Press.

Gottman, John & Silver, Nan (1999). The Seven Principles for Making Marriage Work. New York: Crown Publishers.

Love, Pat (2002). The Truth about Love. New York: Simon and Schuster.

Markman, Howard, Stanley, Scott & Bloomberg, Susan (2002). Fighting for Your Marriage. New York: Wiley/Jossey-Bass.

McCarthy, Barry & McCarthy, Emily (2002). Sexual Awareness. New York: Carroll and Graf.

McCarthy, Barry & McCarthy, Emily (2003). Rekindling Desire. New York: Brunner-Routledge.

Raffel, Lee (1999). Should I Stay or Go? New York: McGraw-Hill.

Spring, Janis (2005). How Can I Forgive You? New York: HarperCollins.

Trafford, Abigail (1992). Crazy Time. New York: Perennial.

Visher, Emily & Visher, John (1991). How to Win as a Stepfamily. New York: Brunner/Mazel.